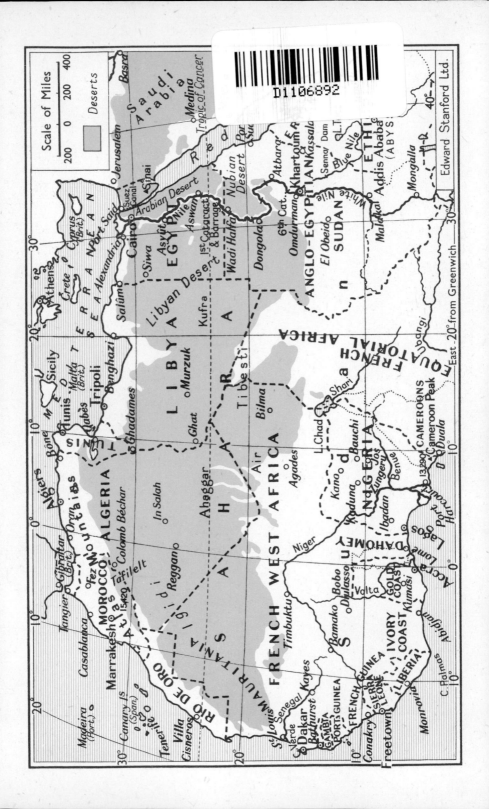

ACROSS THE GREAT DESERTS

An oasis in the Sahara.

ACROSS
THE
GREAT DESERTS

by

P. T. ETHERTON

LUTTERWORTH PRESS
LONDON and REDHILL

First published 1948

This book is produced in
complete conformity with the
authorized economy standard

PRINTED IN GREAT BRITAIN BY THE WHITEFRIARS PRESS LTD.
LONDON AND TONBRIDGE

CONTENTS

LIST OF ILLUSTRATIONS

LIST OF ILLUSTRATIONS

ACKNOWLEDGEMENT

Acknowledgement is made to the following for kind permission to use the photographs of which they hold the copyright :—

Frank C. Betts Ltd., Sir Bede Clifford G.C.M.G., Exclusive News Agency Ltd., Gaumont-British Picture Corporation Ltd., and F. Nink.

INTRODUCTION

What is a desert? The dictionary defines it as an uninhabited and uncultivated tract of land . . . wilderness . . . desolate and barren region. Before I went there I imagined the Sahara to be a wilderness, a sea of sand, with perhaps an oasis here and there and a well of brackish water.

The reality showed me how mistaken I was. The Sahara is certainly not a southern paradise, nor is it a sandy waste : it is a fantastic mixture of desert, dunes, orchards, wheatfields, and high mountains, and oases where palm and date trees can be counted by the thousand, and where you can pick oranges, peaches, and apricots as you might in British Columbia or California.

Then again the Sahara has a great deal to show in the way of romance and primitive charm ; you meet the queerest people on earth there, people who have lived and toiled for hundreds of years amid burning sands, blinding heat, and fierce winds which are of such frequency that you wonder not only how the races have survived, but how there could be reality in this region of desolation. Somehow you cannot imagine life in such an environment.

Far away in the south of Africa is the Kalahari, where we meet the Bushmen, whose cave paintings extend from Africa to the Pyrenees. There is the million-acre game reserve now being set up where the giraffe, lion, antelope, and other game roam undisturbed. And within the limits of the Kalahari are stretches of land that might be devoted to profitable ranching and farming.

Leaving the African continent we pass to the Gobi desert of Mongolia, the second largest in the world, an even greater anomaly than the Sahara. Here is no arid wilderness, for areas of pasture-land for sheep and cattle cover thousands of acres, with waterways, wooded heights, and graceful forests forming a feature of the landscape. Again one wonders how it could ever have been called a desert.

Deserts are an enigma, and in this book we shall study them and see what grim and grave as well as gay and fascinating places they can be.

Let us first look at the physical map of the world and see what deserts there are. You will observe that there are three great barren zones forming broken girdles round the Earth, and covering a tenth of its area.

Ice deserts surround the North and South Poles, and they are known as " cold deserts ". In the north of Europe, Asia, and America they are succeeded by a belt of frozen land called the " Tundra ". This land thaws on the surface in summer and supports a growth of moss, grass, and stunted shrubs. So far, these huge areas have proved useless and unproductive to man because of excessive cold. Scientists and explorers, however, think that there may be deposits of valuable minerals in these snowbound wastes ; but their commercial development lies in the future.

Arid deserts (known as " hot deserts ") occur in all areas of great heat and small rainfall. The northern zone includes the vast Sahara, and the interior of Arabia and Iraq. After a small break with the Persian Gulf comes the Great Salt Desert of Iran, the deserts of Cutch and Thar in India, the deserts of Afghanistan, and, finally, the Desert of Gobi or Shamo. In the United States along the same belt lies the Great Basin of North America.

Horny cacti, the saxaul, with foliage like wire, and the dull-grey sage-bush are characteristic of the scanty plant life.

A similar set of smaller deserts appear in the Southern Hemisphere, near the cooler but drier sides of the continents. The Kalahari in South Africa, the Great Victoria Desert in Australia, and the salt desert of Atacama in South America, form links in the chain.

There is no record of the icy deserts around the two Poles ever having supported human life. In the tundra belt, however, small scattered communities of people live and work. There are, for instance, the Eskimos of Greenland. But it is different with the hot deserts. Within historical times many of these regions were fertile and prosperous, with a large population and advanced civilization. In bygone days much of the Sahara was open grassland. In Iraq and Central Asia archaeologists have excavated the remains of former famous cities, such as Babylon, Nineveh, and Ur. Even in the Gobi there is evidence of much greater communities having once lived there than is the case to-day.

What causes deserts? It is not mainly through total lack of rain, for there is no land on earth so dry that it does not have some rainfall. Possibly the driest desert of all is in Southern Peru, where it may go for seven years or more between rains.

The trouble, however, with desert rainfall is that when it does come it falls in one or two heavy downpours, even in cloudbursts; it is not spread out. Again, certain desert areas have an underlay of porous soil—sand and limestone—which permits rain to percolate underground so freely that the surface is persistently dry. Here the sun's heat falls on barren land, and, not being absorbed by the plants, spends itself in the work of heating air and helping to maintain the permanent winds of the globe. These carry rain to more favoured regions, so, in a sense, the existence of fertile lands is a consequence of deserts.

I have said that it is incorrect to imagine deserts as dreary wastes of sand and monotonous expanses of plains. True, there is much drifting sand and most deserts are either plains or plateaux; but deserts also have many bare, rocky slopes, and even mountains. Where in the middle of desert regions mountains rise high enough, rain falls on their slopes, and streams flow down their valleys. These mountain streams, however, waste away when they reach the sandy plains, or end in salty marshes.

The action of the wind is really more important than lack of water in forming deserts. The fine surface soil is blown away, leaving only the subsoil. This export of dust carries a long way, and soil from the Sahara has even settled in Central Europe and on ships off the West Coast of Africa. This wind action also piles up sand into dunes, some of them several hundred feet in height. These change form—an action which has buried whole cities.

Blown sand alters the course of rivers, and also causes erosion. You can see the results of this erosion in the peculiar shapes of many rocks and hills in the desert. Sometimes a rock will become so corroded at its base that it topples over—and is ground up into more sand and more desert.

There is little doubt that the desert area of the world is increasing. Records show that districts which a century ago were fertile are now waste land. Experts consider that in due course, possibly in a few hundred years, the whole world will become one vast desert. If this does take place man himself will be largely to blame, for at the present time he is the chief creator of deserts. We cannot persist in taking more water out of the ground than goes into it, without creating desert conditions ; and that is what is happening.

These man-made deserts lie all over the earth. Much of China is barren because of the constant cutting down of forests without their replacement. This causes desiccation of the land through the diminution in moisture-bearing winds. Neglect and destruction of this protective vegetation by the Turks is said to be the reason why Iraq, Syria, and Palestine, once " lands flowing with milk and honey ", have become largely arid and barren.

Perhaps the most alarming examples of man-made deserts are to be found in the United States. During the nineteenth century, settlers streamed across this great continent in an endless flood. As they took up land they felled vast stretches of forest to make farms and homesteads, little dreaming that they were destroying Nature's rampart against drought. For years all went well ; the increasing dryness of the soil passed unnoticed, while golden harvests were reaped from the rich, virgin earth. But gradually the bitter spring winds and the parching heat of summer did their work. The level of the subsoil water grew ever lower—in places it fell twenty feet in a century—and the top soil became increasingly hard and dry.

Within the last twenty-five years the result of this forest destruction has become evident. Dust-storms in the area known as the " Dust Bowl " have carried millions of tons of loose soil hundreds of miles away. Soil swept from the western prairies invaded the streets and houses of New York—one thousand five hundred miles distant. Millions of acres of land were devastated, farmhouses buried, orchards and gardens blotted out. It looked as though the Middle West would soon be as barren as the interior of Australia.

But these warnings had their effect, and the government took action. They planted a thousand-mile belt of trees, a hundred

miles wide, with soil-binding grasses, and great dams were built
to conserve water by which the desert lands could be irrigated.
They showed, in fact, that ceaseless activity on the part of man
can save the world from becoming one vast desert.

In addition to existing deserts there are many other areas with
a low rainfall. These form semi-arid regions, often situated on
the borders of deserts, and are potential deserts. One might
almost term them " near-deserts ".

Treeless plains are common in all regions of scanty rainfall,
and one often finds there a great range of temperature. It is
rather alarming to record that semi-arid country occupies over a
quarter of the world's total land surface. Many of these plains
are covered with rich grass during part of the year, but become
deserts of driving dust in the dry season. Deliberate burning
of the old grass is often carried out by the farmers, the purpose
being to stimulate fresh, green grass for the livestock in the
spring. Unfortunately these sweeping fires do much harm, for
they dry up the surface soil still more and kill what bushes and
trees there may be. The slow but sure result is desert conditions.
The fertile prairies of North America, the llanos and pampas of
South America, and the steppes of Russia and Central Asia are
examples of such semi-arid lands.

This desiccation goes on so gradually that the process is barely
perceptible. It simply means that year by year the rainfall is
slightly less, the rivers and the lakes less full of water, and wells
have to be sunk deeper.

Suddenly comes the " capsizing point ". The climate and
land in an affected area change in character. Everything seems
to dry up, the whole land is parched, and dust- and sand-storms
carry on their effective destruction through erosion, excavation,
and burial. There is a repetition, indeed, of the disasters,
already described, that befell the American Middle West.

Even in Britain there are instances of the burying effects of
wind-driven sand. On the Norfolk coast the church of Eccles
was, just over a century ago, almost completely buried. Hundreds of years ago the entire parish of Forvie in Aberdeenshire
was overwhelmed (in this particular disaster zealous Protes-
tants attributed it to the fact that Forvie's inhabitants were
" Papists and grossly ignorant "). In Cornwall there have been

several cases of churches buried completely by sand. Along all European coast-lines one can see places where the drifting sand is turning fertile land slowly and gradually into dunes.

Deserts offer little incentive to human occupation. There may be mineral deposits, but agriculture is only possible with irrigation, and in only a few areas is there sufficient water-supply to provide this. The Nile and the Euphrates are two examples of water-supplies which enable desert areas to support large agricultural populations.

Those people who live in the desert are usually nomads. They lead a life of danger and privation, which makes them hardy, warlike, freedom-loving, and with a contempt for settled life. They use camels—" the ships of the desert "—and for hundreds of years have been traders and caravan leaders. In the Old World these caravans were the chief means of communication between East and West. Many of the Bible descriptions refer to desert life, for Palestine is surrounded by deserts and is on a caravan route.

As already remarked, deserts are an enigma ; in our review of them we shall see how each has its own peculiarities and highlights.

PART ONE   THE SAHARA

THE WAY OF THINGS

THE SAHARA!
What sort of picture does this name convey to you?

Perhaps you imagine a great sea of sand, where the landscape appears so unchanging that no matter how far you travel, you always seem to be in the same place. Perhaps you think of groves of palm-trees and clusters of long black tents and veiled Arab horsemen returning from a raid, or of the men of the famous French Foreign Legion and their many battles with the brave and stubborn tribesmen who inhabit this region.

All these things are familiar enough, but they are only part of the truth. The Sahara is much more than a sea of sand; the people who live there are not all Arabs, nor do they all live in tents; and the British as well as the French have taken part in exploring and opening up the Sahara.

This desert is, indeed, a land of wonders. Did you know that in the Sahara there are:

Cities of salt
Snowstorms
Crocodiles
Punch and Judy shows

and a British equivalent of the French Foreign Legion—the lesser-known but equally praiseworthy Desert Corps of the Libyan Desert?

The truth is that the Sahara contains within its boundaries great mountain ranges almost as high as the Rockies or the Alps, which are snow-covered for part of the year; woods and pastures, where herds of animals graze; running streams containing strange fish and reptiles; and mysterious mud-built cities which few white men have seen: Smara, Tindouf, Taodeni, Ghadames, and Ghat, to name only a few, and, of course, the legendary Timbuktu. There are also great lakes, many miles across; but as the burning sun often turns them into salty marshes, they are not so attractive as lakes usually are.

Travelling across the Sahara, we do encounter great areas of

B 2

sand, forming the familiar ranges of sand dunes depicted in films and books, and also vast level expanses of stones and gravel; but it is the high mountains with their snowfields, and deep valleys carpeted with woods and pastures, which upset our mental picture of the Sahara as being composed only of endless stretches of sand. The mountain called Emi Koussi is over eleven thousand feet high and the granite Ennedi Hills are almost as high; there may be unclimbed peaks which are even higher. In contrast are the areas which are below sea-level.

All this makes the Sahara much more fascinating.

The word " Sahara " means " great desert ". With its three-and-a-half-million square miles it is as large as Europe, without Scandinavia, and larger than the United States.

Its boundaries are but vaguely defined and some are still in dispute.

To the west is the Atlantic, to the north the Atlas Mountains and the Mediterranean, to the east the Red Sea and the Nile, while to the south the Sahara merges into the Sudan and the Niger. From east to west it is about 3,300 miles long and 1,200 miles from north to south.

As we see, the Sahara is many-sided, the greater part being a sea of sand, with high ranges of mountains running to close on ten thousand feet, where the raiders of the desert hide their booty, as the pirates did on various chosen islands in the days of the Spanish Main.

The controlling influence in the Sahara is French; France has done most of the colonizing and is opening up desert ways. To-day in the south where the soil is productive, they are extending their influence, subduing the tribes, building roads and fortified outposts, and carving their way forward with the help of the Foreign Legion, of which, and of its colonizing activities, more will be said later in this book.

The Sahara has been crossed in many ways, mainly by the French, but large areas have never been surveyed. The soil varies from sand to a baked clay surface with stretches of shingle. The habitual yellow or grey contours are relieved by red sandstone, coloured granites, and quartz, with a variety of geologic tints sparkling in the sun.

One may travel for days over a monotonous flat wilderness,

A Saharan oasis may have a few Berber
encampments like this, or—

—be large enough to support a cluster of
    mud-built villages.

and then, quite suddenly, come upon low hills, dunes, ridges, and ravines, out of which a way must be found. It is this broken and highly-coloured ground that must alter our preconceived ideas of a real desert.

In the far south it is still more confusing to the popular idea, for there are areas of ground given over entirely to salt, to which I shall refer later on.

The sun and the elements play tricks. There are miles of loose, sandy soil, which, at first sight, seem like green fields ; indeed, they might be lucerne pastures. Actually, they are stretches of the bitter-tasting gourd and senna plants, through which camels and men flounder as though in marshland.

The oases scattered at wide intervals are sometimes only sufficient for half-a-dozen men and camels, while others have a fluctuating population of anything up to fifty thousand. Some contain five or six villages and range over twenty or thirty square miles, where the villagers gain a scanty livelihood by herding a few flocks, and supplement their income by raids on each other's cattle ; or they may leave their fortified haunts to come out and raid passing commerce. In the days when caravans were traversing the desert with slaves, gold dust, and ivory, business was brisk, but the advance of European authority and the end of slave-trading and ostrich-hunting made it more difficult to earn a living.

On the western borders of the Sahara are towns famous in the fifteenth century and onwards, for here were the lairs of the Barbary pirates, known to the seamen of those days as " Sally Rovers ". They plundered and ravaged the coasts of southern Europe, carried off the lovely girls and women, and put the able-bodied men and boys to work in their sea-coast headquarters.

All this western part of the desert has been conquered and put into order and shape by the French. It is well they have done so, for the Moorish dynasty was a dying and archaic one. Tyranny, cruelty, and corruption were the highlights of administration ; but the French changed all that when their occupation began.

In 1912 a massacre of French troops and subjects took place, and then it was that Lyautey appeared and set out on his career as one of the greatest pro-consuls of our time. He took town after town, and camp after camp, driving the fierce Berber

21

tribesmen headlong into the desert and the hills, and thus laid the foundation of a régime which ranks as a foremost civil and military achievement. Lyautey was a humane soldier, who beat his enemies with their own weapons and won their esteem by declining unfair advantages.

In the west, by the shores of Spanish West Africa, the Sahara runs right to the Atlantic, a grim and inhospitable coastline without harbours, where the sea comes rolling in as a mighty surf. It was in keeping with its sinister reputation that the outstanding thing I saw there was a steamer lying wrecked and forlorn on the beach, the surf thundering over it, and all the fittings stripped by hungry tribesmen.

In all this expanse of country there live only some two-and-a-half-million people, belonging to various races, Arabs, Berbers, Tuaregs, Tebus, and Negroes.

The map shows that the Sahara is divided politically among various countries : Morocco, Algeria, Tunisia, Libya, the Sudan, Egypt, French West Africa, and the little-known Spanish colony of Rio de Oro, or " River of Gold ", as it is called— although there is little gold and no river.

Along the fringes of this part of the desert run various stretches of road and railway, but the greater part of the burning central heart of the Sahara is still crossed only by age-old caravan routes, faint trails in the sand, often marked only by cairns of stones or the bleached bones of men and camels who have died by war or thirst. Wells sometimes mark the cross-roads. These routes were here long before civilization. They were already ancient when Joseph was brought as a slave to Egypt, and those who habitually go over them now are much the same as in Joseph's day. These caravan routes traverse the desert for hundreds, even for thousands of miles, linking oasis with oasis, and town with distant town.

Wherever there is water there is life ; and there are the oases— perhaps just a few palm trees sheltering several of the black camel-hair tents of the desert nomads, or, in some cases, large enough to support several villages of mud-built houses, whose populations cultivate fields of barley and millet and gather the harvest of the date-palms.

Most of the Sahara has now been pacified, but there are still

regions where the tribesmen maintain their independence. These
are gradually growing less, for each year sees the frontiers of
civilization advancing ; and the day is probably not far distant
when the Sahara will be crossed by railway and the wonders of
its little-known cities and palm-groves thrown open to the
world.

Come now to the heart of the Sahara.

You are in the dominion of the sun, whose rays strike down
like the blast of a furnace. You live in an atmosphere of sand
and heat, with winds that sweep up the sand and turn the desert
into an inferno. This wind may blow for days ; in no place is
it more pitiless or penetrating, blinding the eyes, cracking the
skin, conquering everything. The heat is like nothing imagin-
able. It is more than just heat : it is a force that kills. By nine
o'clock in the morning the surrounding landscape becomes a
blue-white glare which makes the eyes ache to look at it.

The Tanezruft Desert, the central part of the Sahara, known as
" The Land of Thirst ", is said to be one of the hottest spots on
earth. At midday the temperature may be 125 degrees in the
shade, perhaps even higher, and by midnight it may have
dropped to fifty degrees, or even to below freezing-point. The
extreme change in temperature—the cold and frost of the nights—
is another thing not always associated with the Sahara.

Rain is rare ; in some places seven to ten years have gone by
without it. Yet, even here, without the slightest indication of
what is coming, a cloud or two will appear far off in the sky.
Then from the heavens comes heat lightning ; bigger clouds loom
on the horizon. There is a rush for every pot and vessel to catch
the priceless rain. All sorts of receptacles are improvised, for
the chance may only happen once in ten years. The camp
becomes a waterworks ; there is gaiety and delight, for the
rain has come. Years will pass before it comes again.

After the rain is the best time for travelling. The atmosphere
is soft, and the days are clear and beautiful ; but the magic moment
passes. Soon the burning sun returns and you feel no longer
the invigoration and joy of life. You are again in the inter-
minable wastes, going on and on. . . .

You may leave your camp at dawn as the sun climbs into a
hard, blue sky, casting shadows from the date palms of the oasis—

if you are lucky enough to find one. The sand quivers in the haze, the hours drag on till the peaceful cool of the evening. You halt in a landscape of sand and sorrow. How delightful it then is to stretch out, forget the toil of the day, and look at the stars on their voyage!

All this was here long, long before your coming. It will be here long, long after your going. . . . .

But the desert is not always at peace. There is the sand-storm which springs up with devastating swiftness. Travel is then impossible. All you can do is to turn the camels round, make a zariba of them and the baggage, and crouch under cover until the storm has passed. The camels kneel with their backs to the wind and sand; baggage and loads form a wall against the fury.

Far away on the horizon black clouds seem to come out of the earth. A light and tolerant breeze sweeps over the camp. It is the advance guard of the sand-storm, which can now be defined, much nearer, rushing on with terrifying speed.

Hoarse voices are shouting in the roar of the storm, the sand and grit are blinding everyone; there is a profound darkness all around, with the storm sweeping and striking in every direction.

Then comes a sudden lull, the wind dies down, the hurricane passes on, and the sky grows clear again. The peace of the Sahara is restored.

§

IN THE GREAT DUNES

A FAMOUS artist once told me that when trying to paint a mirage he saw a gigantic figure striding towards him across the sand. Many men might have fled. But the artist, laying aside his brushes, rose to his feet, preparing to shake hands with the spectre; which he soon discovered to be himself.

"Never have I felt so great—and so small," he told me.

I tell this story as an introduction to yet another puzzle of the Sahara : the riddle of the dunes.

The sand dunes are a mystery in themselves; some are only

Footprints in a sea of sand—but not all of
the Sahara is like this : the picture over the
page is of a part of the same desert.

The sun-bleached bones of a camel mark the
route a caravan has taken.

a few feet high, others may be as much as a hundred feet, each composed of that devastating, all-pervading sand that has swallowed up once-flourishing cities.

These dunes have originated weird and ghostly stories—creepy tales of fairies and gnomes peculiar to the superstitious. Certainly one cannot marvel at the legends, for the expanse of sand has a dismal and depressing effect upon the traveller. Where the winds are of unusual frequency, especially in the southern parts of the desert, the dunes seem to mount up in successive walls, with flat spaces between them twenty or thirty yards wide. Thus you have a long succession of corridors, not always straight, for they bend and wind according to how the wind has directed and formed them.

It is eerie being among those dunes ; you seem shut off and in a ghostly prison, with no sign of human, animal, or vegetable life, no sound of bird or beast, nothing whatever to relieve the sepulchral silence. We can well understand why the desert people believe such places to be the abode of demons and evil spirits.

Then there are the singing and the drumming sands, especially in the sandhills and dunes of the Ouargla district, one of the strangest tracts of country in the world, even for the Sahara. Guy de Maupassant, in one of his thrilling stories, tells of a curious phenomenon which, though familiar to travellers in those parts, has never been explained.

We all know what the smooth level sands of a sea beach are like, running on and on interminably. We can picture in our minds the ocean turned to sand in the middle of a hurricane. Imagine a tempest without sound, and billows of yellow sand that never move. To the height of mountains they rise, these irregular waves of all shapes and sizes, surging like the ungovernable waters of the ocean, but vaster, and streaked like watered silk. The pitiless rays of the devastating southern sun bear straight down upon that raging sea lying there without sound or motion.

A journey across these dunes is one of continual ascent and descent, without a moment's respite or a vestige of shade.

One day a party of men and camels were moving through these sandhills. Overcome with heat and fatigue, parched with thirst as the burning desert itself, they rode on in silence. Suddenly one of them uttered a cry . . . everyone halted ; they remained rooted to the spot surprised by that strange sound of drumming in the sandhills. From somewhere near at hand, but in a direction difficult to determine, came the roll of a drum. Its beating was distinct, now loud, now dying away, now resuming its weird tattoo. The party looked at one another in horror, and one of the desert men said, "Death is upon us." As he spoke one of them fell headlong from his mount, struck down by sunstroke.

For some time the others laboured in vain to save his life, and still that phantom drum filled their ears with its monotonous, intermittent, and baffling throbbing. And there they were . . . with the dead body of their comrade, in that sun-baked hollow between the sandhills, six hundred miles from the nearest French settlement, with that rapid, mysterious drumming echoing in their ears.

Nobody knows what the mysterious drum is. Travellers who have often been startled by this singular sound are generally of the opinion that it is caused by sand scudding before the wind and brushing against tufts of dry grass, the echo being intensified and multiplied to a prodigious volume by the valley formation of that desert region. It has been observed that the phenomenon always occurs near small plants burnt up by the sun and as hard as parchment. According to this theory the drum was simply a sort of sound mirage, nothing more.

§

TRAVELLING IN THE SAHARA

THE Sahara is not yet overcrowded as a holiday resort, but travelling across the desert to-day is not quite so difficult as many people imagine. There are regular motor-coach services which run several times a week between the main centres of civilization. Yet it was only in 1922 that the first motor-car expedition travelled over great stretches of the desert.

Crossing the desert will always be a good test of a car. Those used on the regular transportation services have six sets of double wheels and carry a dozen passengers. They seem to be able to climb the steepest dunes, and seldom get stuck in the soft sand. When a car *is* held up, all the passengers have to alight to dig out the wheels and push. You get a thrill when the car charges a lofty sand-ridge and you find yourself on the summit, looking down almost vertically. The design of these cars seems to enable them to negotiate any gradient.

It would be easy to get lost among the sea of sand, and a desert guide has to be carried. To the ordinary traveller there seem to be no landmarks for miles at a time to assist in judging direction. The French Government has placed a series of small concrete pyramids about six feet high at intervals of about half a mile along the main routes, but the incessant sand-storms often cover them. Except on the flat stretches it is seldom that one pillar can be seen from another. Occasionally the debris left by other travellers marks the route, but little is wasted in the desert, and even old tin cans have a value that makes them worth picking up. Further, the constantly-moving sand can wash a track clean like the tide on a beach.

There are few signs of animal life on these long journeys; occasionally you see a gazelle and wonder what it lives on. The only travellers likely to be encountered are desert nomads, travelling with their household goods on camels, as they have done for centuries.

The camel caravans, which have traversed the Sahara periodically for untold generations, take their leisurely course along traditional routes determined by the presence of the oases. Beyond these more-or-less habitable spots, where there is water and some vegetation, lie great expanses of waterless, arid country which until recent years were entirely unmapped and unexplored. During the present century, the French, impatient for exact knowledge of their African domain and for more rapid communications across it, have penetrated deeper and deeper into the unknown Sahara. They have ploughed their way over it in motor trucks fitted with caterpillar wheels. They have flown above it and traced ranges of dunes and mountains and ancient water-courses upon maps previously characterized by blanks. They have drilled artesian wells and cultivated crops where formerly there was nothing but dry sand. And they now look forward to the day when one will be able to ride right across the forbidding Sahara in a railway Pullman car, sipping iced drinks beside an electric fan all the way from the Mediterranean to the Gulf of Guinea, travelling from Paris to Timbuktu in four or five days.

The Sahara is not the endless desert which it used to be, for its relation to man has been changed, first by the motor-car, and secondly, and even more radically, by the aeroplane. Now one can cover by plane in a short day's flying a distance which would take a man on a camel six weeks to traverse.

Imagine that you look at the Sahara from the air.

Shortly before the recent war I flew over the western Sahara in a Zeppelin as the guest of Dr. Eckener. It was a remarkable land we were looking down on. The camels that we saw cannot claim to be the most ancient animals of North-West Africa : the patient donkey is the domestic animal that can really call itself the oldest inhabitant. Coming here long before the camel-man and the Moslem faith, it ambled over this country even before the three wise men rode into Bethlehem. The Moors, the Berbers, and the Kabyles, whom we saw below us in the desert, were tending their flocks as they did decades ago, and time had not altered or varied the picture.

One could see that the Sahara was no place for Lilliputians. For centuries civilization has recoiled in terror from North Africa, with its sand hot enough to burn shoe leather and its thirsty horizons which have swallowed up whole caravans. Now, what with the proposed railway and the irrigation schemes, it is being beleaguered and forced to yield up some of its secrets. Up in the air we talked about the possibilities of the future.

The story of the awakening of the Sahara, under the latest conditions of development and transport, is as wonderful as any tale of Giant-Killer or Sleeping Beauty. It is, in fact, the story of the slaying of the greatest giant left alive, and one before whom Europeans have recoiled in apprehension.

The desert has always been inimical to men of the west ; the wind blowing from Africa out of the dried-up dusty attics of history has chilled the blood and pinched the face of the hardy northerner, accustomed to the enjoyment of his meat and drink and the soft glances of rivers and trees. There is something contrary, opposed to his heritage and instincts, about places where good liquor induces madness and distances mean death, something overwhelming and inert that made the very eagles of Rome and Napoleon droop on their standards. From Carthage to the conquering Moors, and the stranglehold of the Barbary corsairs, the Sahara has brooded like an evil genie over Southern Europe. You cannot look at it comfortably without dark glasses, and even then you want to rub your eyes.

The railroad is going to press southward ; from the Sudan to Senegal, from the Nile to the Niger, a network of communication is springing up. Cars are already traversing uninhabited portions of the landscape during winter, though during the excessive summer heat motor transport proves to be well-nigh impossible. With the close of this long and deadly struggle the trans-Saharan railway may soon be an accomplished fact. Timbuktu itself is no longer a byword among byways.

But one will not say that the Sahara has been really conquered until this trans-Saharan railway, which now juts out forlornly into the northern fringe of the desert, has been extended to Gao, on the Niger River east of Timbuktu. The motor-trail to this town was blazed by the Estienne brothers, who founded the Trans-Saharan Transport Company. There were two stopping-places along this route, Reggan and Bidon 5. The first place had a modern hotel standing in an oasis ; Bidon 5, on the other hand, consisted merely of a white-enamelled petrol pump with two old bus shelters beside it for travellers to sleep in.

Airmen of the Sahara follow the outline of the motor route, which is here sketched by empty petrol drums set up on edge, one every three miles. Motor-cars may not venture far from the trail, but aircraft are linked by wireless. When an airman is on his way from one desert centre to another, the wireless operators at the airfields know when he takes off from one place and when he is expected at the next.

Sand-storms, already described as one of the worst dangers to the desert traveller, are also a danger to flyers across the Sahara. These storms give little warning of their approach. The sky suddenly goes a dirty-yellow colour, and the aeroplane must either get above the storm or make a hasty landing. It is not always possible to rise above the storm area, which may extend upward for several thousand feet with a fury that makes flying almost impossible.

Experienced desert flyers carry shovels, ropes, and sandbags. If they do have to make a hasty landing, they hastily shovel sand into the bags and tie them to the wings and tail of the machine. Then they cover the engine and plug the exhaust pipes, and finally shelter in a trench, staying there with water-tank and food until the storm has passed over. These precautions are necessary, for the terrific wind will wreck an aircraft in a few minutes unless it has something to weight it down.

Timbuktu, that remote and mysterious city in the heart of Africa, once regarded as a symbol of the inaccessible, may soon be linked to the outer world by railway. One will presently be able to travel there by swift Diesel-electric train. Then two thousand miles of track will span the Sahara, and the world's worst desert will be conquered.

Construction is already under way. The railway is being built simultaneously from north and south, and the already existing line from Dakar, on the Atlantic coast, will be linked with a projected northward extension to In-Tassit, on the edge of the desert near Timbuktu. At the same time a northern section joining up with the Algerian railways is being driven southward to the town of Béni Abbes, situated among the great sand dunes. The long central section in between, yet to be built, must cross the desert known as " The Land of Thirst ". Bridging that fearful desolation will probably be the hardest task ever attempted by railroad engineers.

One thing that the engineers will not have to worry about is water, the great enemy of railroad construction. The Sahara is so dry that metal sleepers with concrete ends are being used. On the level plains of the central desert is a solid surface of stone and gravel which offers a natural base for motor road or railway. The actual construction, according to engineers, can take place at a fairly rapid rate. In the Anglo-Egyptian Sudan a railway was laid at the rate of four miles a day, another in Siberia at the rate of six miles a day. In Arizona, Russian Turkestan, and Australia, railways have been built across deserts.

Fuel and water for driving the railway engines is a problem. Steam-engines require much water. Probably Diesel-electric engines, which use little water and can give up to three thousand horse-power, will be the solution. The water obtained from boreholes in the heart of the desert contains too much magnesia and sulphates to be used in boilers. But all these difficulties can be overcome.

The Saharan railway was talked of as far back as 1875. The French Government sent an expedition to explore the proposed route, but its members were killed by the desert tribesmen. Some years later a private company was formed to build a railway linking Algeria with the River Niger, but nothing came of it. After the First World War the scheme was discussed again, and engineers explored the desert to discover the best way of carrying railway tracks across it. Powerful commercial rivals managed to get the idea postponed, and it was not until 1941 that the French Government declared that construction had begun.

For what reason is the French Government spending enormous sums of money in what is traditionally regarded as one of the most barren and worthless regions of the globe? The answer is that such a railway would be a vital link with the Niger. The Niger Valley is potentially one of the greatest sources of natural wealth in Africa. Rubber, wheat, tobacco, rice, cotton, coffee—in fact, practically every plant necessary to modern civilization—can be grown there successfully. With proper irrigation the region could become a second Nile Valley. In war, also, the railway would be of immense value, as it would be possible to move bodies of troops to strategic points very quickly.

It is also suggested that the railway might be prolonged into Nigeria to connect with the British railway system, and through the Cameroons and French Equatorial Africa into the Belgian Congo. The Belgians have expressed keen interest. Adjoining the Belgian Congo on the east are the British possessions of Uganda, Kenya, and Tanganyika, the former German East Africa, representing, with the French colonies to the west and north, an immense and little-developed tropical area, abounding in a variety of raw materials and capable, perhaps, of becoming a great market for European goods.

SECRET CITIES OF THE SAHARA

FOR hundreds of years romantic stories of strange, unknown cities and fabulous riches lured travellers into the burning heart of the desert. Names such as Timbuktu, the Niger, Rio de Oro, the Ahaggar Mountains, Air, and Tibesti, and tales of cities of salt and rivers of gold and fierce veiled fighting-men, attracted European explorers and merchants, so that they were willing to risk the perils of the desert in order to bring back knowledge of these strange, unknown lands.

All kinds of people have taken a hand in the opening-up of the Sahara, from the Phœnicians and Romans to the airmen and tankmen who fought there in the Second World War. Moslem pilgrims and travellers, English and German explorers, French missionaries and soldiers, gradually penetrated the desert barriers and brought back authentic accounts of what they had seen. Thus the world first heard of the high mountains of the Central Sahara, with their woods and streams and snowfields, of the strange rivers which rose amid the snow and died away in the burning sands, of the veiled Tuaregs who were believed to be descended from lost bands of Crusaders, of the ruined cities of great empires which flourished when the Sahara was a fertile, green land.

It was the legendary wealth of these lost cities of forgotten empires which first attracted white men, and led to the opening up of the great oases : Tuat, Tidikelt, Tafilet, Siwa, Kufra, and many another. The whole story is too long to be told in detail here, but that of one lost city—Timbuktu—must be told, for it epitomizes the history of the Sahara. For a thousand years romantic tales of the desert capital reached the shores of the Mediterranean, but though many tried to reach the fabulous city it was left to René Caillié, a shoemaker, to achieve this feat.

There is something almost unbelievable about the story of René Caillié, the French shoemaker's apprentice, who was the first white man to reach Timbuktu and return to tell the story. Expedition after expedition, equipped with government support

A caravan on the move.

A sand-storm in the Sahara, photographed
from a distance of one mile.

and all the latest scientific knowledge, failed to reach the mysterious city, and it was left to poor, obscure Caillié to succeed. Without education, official backing, or much scientific knowledge, this small, frail young man, equipped with only a few trade articles and enough personal luggage to last from Saturday to Monday, left the coast of Guinea on April 19, 1827, and pushed on across deserts and jungles until he reached Timbuktu exactly a year and a day later, afterwards proceeding northward across the Sahara to Tangier. Thus he accomplished the longest single journey ever made across Africa. He went the whole way disguised as a Moslem pilgrim, and a single mistake at any moment might well have meant his death.

Apart from the fact that he accomplished one of the most remarkable feats of modern exploration, Caillié is probably the most outstanding example known to history of a man with a fixed idea. His story is one of unceasing struggle to make a dream come true. Can the annals of exploration show another case of a boy in a small French village, who, without money, education, or encouragement, became possessed of a longing to reach a remote, undiscovered city in the heart of Africa, and without wavering, and with a determination akin to madness, concentrated all his efforts in that direction, enduring every hardship and setback, until he achieved his goal?

" I will go to Timbuktu! " How often as a boy he made this declaration to his playmates at the village school at Mauze, a hundred miles north of Bordeaux, where he was born on November 19, 1799. Jeers and ridicule failed to destroy his longing to see Africa. It was not his ambition which was laughed at, for many practical, hard-headed business men had a similar idea. Timbuktu was regarded as the great trading-centre of Africa, at the junction of the Sahara and the Niger, " where the camel and the canoe meet ". It was believed to be a rich city, the capital of a black empire, the headquarters of the gold trade. The man who could reach the place and establish trade relations with its inhabitants would be doing a great service to his country. But no Christian had ever reached the city and returned to tell about it.

Discovering Timbuktu was a matter of practical business ; but that poor René Caillié, whose father had died in prison while serving a twelve-year sentence for stealing six francs, should accomplish such a feat, was laughable. The Cailliés were poor, and René's mother had a hard struggle to maintain her six children. She died when he was nine, and he was sent to live with his grandmother, who apprenticed him to the local shoemaker. He loathed the work, and one day in April, 1816, after a quarrel with his master, he left the shoemaker's shop with sixteen francs in his pocket and started out for Africa. He was a frail, earnest lad of sixteen, and it was to take him twelve years to reach Timbuktu.

The French Government had started a " Plan of Colonization " to open up West Africa, so René shipped as officer's servant at a wage of eighteen francs a month. Twenty-three days later he reached Dakar in Senegal. How thrilled he was to visit native settlements, watch strange tribes, and see the vast Sahara ! Jealously he heard of English expeditions setting out to reach Timbuktu, and probably breathed a sigh of relief when they were repulsed by hostile tribesmen.

Hearing that an English expedition led by a Major Gray wanted men, he set out to walk three hundred miles to the Gambia River to join the party, but collapsed exhausted at a French post. The friendly commander nursed him, and then sent him to work at Guadeloupe, in the West Indies. Here he read Mungo Park's journal, describing his attempts to reach the Niger, and, fired with fresh enthusiasm, René promptly set out for Africa again. He was now nineteen, and possessed only the clothes he stood up in. " Nothing discouraged me," he wrote : " everything seemed possible to my adventurous spirit, and luck seemed to be serving my destiny."

He managed to join Gray's party, and spent four months exploring the desert with them before they were turned back by hostile tribesmen. Then, desperately ill, penniless and friendless, he returned to St. Louis, capital of Senegal, where he became a cook. His experiences had taught him that large expeditions were too slow and cumbersome ; their very size and quantity of equipment made them open to attack and plundering by native potentates. The man who would reach Timbuktu must do it alone and in disguise. First, however, he must grow strong.

For the next four years he worked at a wine-merchant's office in Bordeaux, and then, in 1824, set out on his third journey to Africa. He was now twenty-four years old and had a small stock of goods which he intended to trade with the natives. He planned to reach Timbuktu disguised as a Moslem ; so, in order to learn native ways, he spent nearly a year living among the savage Moors of Senegal.

They were the most feared people in North Africa, the old saying being that " The Moor's tent casts its shade over nothing decent except the horse." Caillié learned to endure the hardships and discomforts of native life, hunger and thirst, long marches, and the terrible desert climate. Because of this hard preliminary training he was eventually able to withstand the rigours of the journey.

Efforts to get help from the governor of Senegal were fruitless, so he worked as overseer on indigo plantations. Disgusted, he took ship to Freetown, Sierra Leone, then considered the deadliest place on earth, and became director of the indigo plantations there. He decided that it was useless waiting for someone to help him ; he must pay for the expedition himself. He began to save all the money he could, having learned that the French Geographical Society was offering a reward of ten thousand francs to the man who first brought back accurate information about Timbuktu. Meanwhile, another English expedition, under the command of Major Laing, set off to reach the forbidden city.

At long last Caillié had saved two thousand francs, which he considered enough for his purpose. With this he bought trade goods : gunpowder, paper, tobacco, glassware, handkerchiefs, knives, and mirrors. His only scientific instruments were two pocket compasses. English friends gave him a medicine outfit, and showed him the graves of men who had died while trying to reach Timbuktu.

Caillié, now aged twenty-seven, was as determined as ever, and on April 19, 1827, he set out. He was dressed as a Moslem, and posed as an Egyptian named Abdallahi who had been taken to France as a child, then to Senegal, where he had been released by his master. He was now returning to Egypt by way of Timbuktu. It was a dangerous deception, for had the natives realized that he was a Christian it would have meant a dreadful death for him.

c 2

At first he accompanied a caravan bound for Cambaya, which they reached in twenty-two days, averaging eleven or twelve miles a day. They crossed fever-haunted marshes, swam rushing rivers, and climbed mountain passes. Caillié was attacked by monkeys, and nearly drowned in a torrent; he suffered from fever, fleas, mosquitoes, and heat. Yet he managed to keep a diary of his journey, writing it on the backs of pages of the Koran.

In two months he crossed the Niger and reached the walled city of Kankan. The priests tested his knowledge of the Moslem faith and accepted him as a genuine pilgrim. He had to listen to the name of Christ being reviled, and to tell of cruelties practised by the Christians. His guide sought to steal his trade goods; so he joined another caravan, but a poisoned foot prevented him from travelling.

He remained at a village called Tieme for five months, with despair in his heart, and half-dead with scurvy. His only food was boiled rice or peanuts with an occasional stewed mouse; the people were too poor to eat roast dog or rat, though they sometimes had caterpillars, ants, or locusts. There were no tinned foods for explorers in those days. Finally he was well enough to travel again.

On the two months' journey to Jenné he suffered from colds, having to sleep outdoors during the cold winter nights. Jenné was an amazing town, surrounded by a moat, and with a better system of sewers and toilets than many a European city. He was the first white man to visit the town, which thereafter remained unknown until 1893.

Caillié traded his umbrella for a passage on a pirogue, one of the big Niger canoes, some of which were a hundred feet long, carried eighty tons, and were made of small planks *sewn* together with palm-leaf ropes. The craft was loaded with slaves, bags of millet, kola nuts, honey, and peanuts, with a crew of sixteen, and had a speed of two miles an hour. Under the blazing African sun they journeyed down the Niger, which in places was twenty-four miles wide. Tuareg raiders came out in boats and took toll of the passing ships.

After a voyage of twenty-six days they reached Kabara, the port of Timbuktu. Exactly a year after beginning his journey

Caillié started across the five miles of sandy waste which lay between the river and the city. On the morning of April 20, 1828, he saw the buildings of Timbuktu just ahead, and knew that his long quest was ended.

Oddly enough, Timbuktu welcomed Caillié in friendly fashion, for news of the Egyptian pilgrim had already reached there, and a kindly merchant lent him a house to live in. It says much for Caillié's tact and knowledge that never once was his identity challenged ; no one doubted that he was a pious Moslem striving to get back to his homeland. Though often insulted, robbed, and starved, this was no more than might happen to any wandering Moslem pilgrim, and he never suffered the injuries, slavery, or death which was the lot of many European explorers.

Caillié described Timbuktu as an unwalled collection of sand-coloured houses and narrow streets clustered about the Great Mosque, with the desert reaching to its doors. There were no trees, grass, or greenery. The city produced nothing, but acted as a clearing-house for the products of the trans-Saharan trade routes. For hundreds of years it had been rich and powerful, the capital of an African empire, but when Caillié reached it its glory had departed and it was in decay. Yet it was still the most renowned city in Africa.

Caillié remained fifteen days in Timbuktu, being entertained by local notables, and, under pretence of meditating in the tower of the mosque, was able to make geographical observations and sketches. He learned that Laing, the English explorer, had reached the city twenty months before him, but had been strangled and buried out in the desert. Caillié realized that it was one thing to reach the secret city and quite another to get safely back to France with his information. He *must* get back to civilization ; and return he did, though it meant a journey across the Sahara in midsummer, and an equally dangerous one through fanatical Morocco. Finally, on September 7, 1828, his long journey ended at the French Consul's house in Tangier, and a few days later he was on board a ship bound for home.

He became the most talked-of man in France, received the French Geographical Society's award, was made a Chevalier of the Legion of Honour, and dined with the King of France.

At long last all his dreams of fame and fortune had come true.

As for Timbuktu, it was officially occupied by the French in 1894. Though it has now shrunk to the status of a small town, there is a glamour about its name which will never fade.

§

PEOPLE OF THE DESERT

WHAT of the people who live in the Sahara? They are not all Arabs, as is popularly supposed, but are mostly Berbers, who lived in North Africa long before the coming of the Arabs. The old name for them was Moors, and though they are still often called by this name, that title is really confined to persons of Arab blood who live in the cities of North Africa.

Where the Berbers themselves came from no one knows, for they were living in North Africa when history began. It has been suggested that they are of Celtic origin, like the Scots and Irish, for they still retain names such as M'Tougi, M'Guild, and M'Goun. Neither Romans nor Arabs were ever able to conquer them completely, but both employed them in their armies, for, as we shall see, the Berber is a fine fighting-man. Berber warriors marched over the Alps with Hannibal to the gates of Rome, and the armies with which the Arabs conquered Spain were largely composed of Berbers. The name of Hannibal is still to be found among them.

It is astounding the things these Berber warriors accomplished. It was long after Mohammed's death in A.D. 654 that the "holy war" commenced for the expansion of the Moslem faith, and once that faith was established in North Africa, the Berbers made a beginning in Europe with the invasion of Spain.

The deeds of the Berbers are an essential part of our story and a remarkable example of the strength that came out of the desert— this conquest of part of Europe by the Berbers, a fighting power that developed into a hundred years of splendour; it came about by the new religion and the new vitalizing force created by

Mohammed. He was the man who started it and held aloft the torch that eventually flamed from Spain to China, through a large part of Asia, and embraced all North Africa. Morocco and the Sahara were the linch pin.

It was from Morocco and the desert that Islam received its greatest impetus outside Arabia. The Berbers seemed to think it would be easy to subjugate the Continent. Their army was directed by the Sultan of Morocco and under the command of Jebel Tariq. To secure his communications with North Africa, Jebel Tariq founded the fortress of Gibraltar; he built a fort half-way up the north-western slope of the Rock which commanded a wide area along the bay. A square tower, it still stands splendid and defiant, and is known as the Moorish castle.

These Berbers, these men of the desert, who came out of the unknown and were destined to make history in Europe, were commanded by men Napoleonic in their conception and knowledge of war. They did not embark lightly on a great and risky enterprise.

Jebel Tariq had studied Cæsar's Commentaries, as Napoleon did eleven hundred years later, and he also knew his Socrates. Socrates had said : " A general must know how to assure his men their food, and the stores of every kind requisite for war. In forming his plan of campaign he must have originality, common sense, and the wit and energy to carry them through. He must be observant, tireless, clever, kindly, and cruel ; simple and crafty ; a watchman and a robber, lavish and miserly, generous and stingy ; he must be rash and conservative. All these and many other qualities, natural and acquired, he must have. He must know tactics, for a disorderly army is no more an army than a heap of building materials is a house."

The Berbers followed this advice. They decided to send over a small detachment to the southern shores of Spain. Accordingly a mixed force of five hundred horse and foot set sail, landing near Algeciras. It met with no opposition, and the Berbers spread out, raided the countryside, and then re-embarked to report to the Sultan.

In the next year twelve thousand men assembled near what is now Tangier. It even had a covering force of warships.

This invasion in A.D. 711 is an early example of an expeditionary force crossing the sea, an amphibious undertaking of which the modern counterpart was the landing in Normandy in 1944, more than twelve hundred years later. But in 711 it was a different proposition, for lack of knowledge of the sea and its dangers kept the people to the land. When they had to go afloat they preferred to follow the coastline, moving cautiously from one point to the next, and always keeping within sight of land, navigating only during daylight and taking refuge at night on the shore, where they could be sheltered from the winds and the reefs.

Ships were propelled by fifty or sixty rowers ; the boats were single-deckers, with the prow raised like the neck of a swan. If the breeze was light or contrary the human motive force sent the boat through the water by strength of arm, but with a following wind they hoisted a square sail made from Egyptian linen.

These transports carried three or four hundred persons. Among their armament was a kind of forerunner of the German *Flammenwerfer*, and they also used catapults, and earthen jars filled with snakes and scorpions to be launched among the enemy.

The force landed at Gibraltar, where they encountered the Spanish troops, who were a raw and undisciplined force. The Berbers soon prevailed ; and their victory, when followed up, left them in possession of almost the whole of Spain.

So began the Berber infiltration. But it was not to be for all time. Slowly through the years the Spaniards gathered strength. The French joined in, for the Berbers had pushed to the Pyrenees, which they crossed into France. In a great battle at Poitiers they came up against the French forces. For six days the Berber commander manœuvred, and on the morning of the seventh he attacked, and was heavily repulsed. It was the beginning of the end of Moorish domination in Europe ; and the Berbers retired across the Pyrenees to Spain, from which, however, they were not finally driven until 1462.

As the Arabs swept across North Africa, from the eighth century onwards, many of the Berber tribes preferred to retreat into the Sahara rather than submit to the conquerors. From them descended such desert tribes as the Tuaregs and the Blue Moors, who have become so accustomed to living in this inhospitable region that they would not live anywhere else. The tribes

Two contrasting studies in sand : this, an
aerial view of the desert ; and, over the
page, the heart of the dunes.

Two ancient means of irrigation in the Sahara : the canal, and
the primitive, camel-worked well.

living on the fringes of the Sahara are of mixed descent, those on the north having intermarried with the Arabs, those on the south with the Negroes.

The Berbers are of the white races, for it is only exposure to the burning sun which makes them look dark-skinned. Many are as fair-skinned as Europeans, and blue eyes and fair hair are not uncommon among them. In fact, another theory of their origin is that they are the descendants of the Vandals, the Germanic race who founded a kingdom in North Africa in the fifth century and who vanish mysteriously from the pages of history a century or so later.

The Berber is an independent sort of man and has always been " agin the government ", whatever that government may be. He fights for the sheer love of it, and many Berbers took part in the First and Second World Wars. Although brave and cruel, he is a sportsman in his way, and bears no resentment towards those who have defeated him in war.

Berbers differ from Arabs in many respects, in their methods of fighting, in the treatment of their womenfolk, and principally in their attitude towards modern civilization. Like the European, the Berber has a mechanical turn of mind, and is extremely interested in aircraft, engines, and machinery ; whereas the Arabs regard these things as the work of the devil. The Berbers despise the Arabs as cowards, while the Arabs regard the Berbers as savages.

Although many of the Berber tribes live in tents, Arab-fashion, they are really a race of house-dwellers, living in villages of stone or mud, or in big, many-turreted houses, which are actually castles.

These castles of the northern Sahara are unique ; there is nothing to compare with them. Wherever there is water, and wherever there is life, you see these red-tinted strongholds, built of *tabia* or native concrete. With their thick walls and tapering Babylonian towers, their massive donjons and barbicans, they are one of the striking forms of present-day African architecture. They are really fortified communal storehouses. The members of a Transhumant Berber tribe, who are nomads for one half of the year and farmers for the other, cannot carry about with them everything they possess, especially reserves of food. So each family group has its own particular fortress, which it leaves in charge of trusted guards during its pastoral wanderings.

The *tabia* of which the buildings is constructed is composed of earth, lime, and pebbles pounded together. When the foundations of a house are laid out, moulds made of planks arranged in parallel rows are filled with this material, which is then pounded into a solid mass. This rapidly hardens into a strong, durable building material which will last for years in the rainless desert country.

After the first section of the wall is completed, the planks are moved higher and the process is repeated. The strong towers, sometimes seventy feet high, are erected without the aid of any mechanical appliances. The roofs consist of wooden beams covered by dried canes, plastered stiff with beaten clay.

These strongholds are usually square or oblong in shape, protected by battlemented walls and towers, and surrounded by a wide stretch of open land affording no cover for enemies. The gates are usually double, having a sharp turn half-way, so that attackers cannot see what lies inside. As a rule they lead into an open square surrounded by houses. Narrow streets, mere tunnels with houses built over them, criss-cross this human warren.

The houses are usually several storeys high. The ground floor serves as stables and store-rooms, while the first floor, reached by sloping corridor instead of stairs, acts as living quarters ; above are the granaries. The watch-towers contain galleries loopholed for defence.

Outside the *ksar*, or fortified tribal house, is the *nuadder*, or threshing-floor. The grain is flung down upon this wide mud platform and then trampled upon by horses and mules driven round and round. Straw and chaff are thrown into the air, to be blown away by the wind, so that finally only the seed remains.

In these mud strongholds the old patriarchal mode of life prevails, and when invited inside you sit cross-legged on a reed mat beside a glistening samovar and drink the three cups of mint tea required by Berber etiquette. There is often considerable difference in the social and political organization of the tribes ; many are ruled by *Kaids*, or lords, who exercise despotic authority ; others are organized as republics.

A Saharan oasis is criss-crossed by canals and conduits, dividing it into small fields, which are again divided into plots ten to twenty yards wide, separated by low banks of earth. The canals are raised slightly above the surrounding fields, enabling them to be more quickly irrigated. The crops of barley, maize, and millet are grown under the shelter of the palm trees, to protect them from the sun.

The oases depend for their existence upon the rivers which rise in the high mountains of the Sahara and flow down into the heart of the desert before their waters die away in the thirsty sands. During the heat of midsummer the rivers shrink in volume until only pools, or perhaps only the dry bed of the stream, are left, so that it is necessary to conserve all the water possible.

Save for oases in the river-beds, this northern country appears to be absolute desert. Owing to the rivers' having carved deep canyons below the surface, the oases, with their fields and castles, are invisible until you reach the cliff-tops. Upon the width of the strip of land lying between the cliffs bordering the river depends the number of the population.

Water played an important part in Berber warfare. Villages lying a mile or two from a river depended upon canals for their water supply, and the diverting of this canal to another community naturally led to war. When a *ksar* was besieged the attackers first tried to cut off the water supply, thus forcing the besieged to come out into the open. Conversely, a canal would be dug along the walls of the stronghold and in a few hours the building would start to crumble into ruins, *tabia* being unable to withstand the effects of moisture.

To obviate an enemy's seizing the canals, watch-towers were built on mounds along the banks. These square-loopholed forts were garrisoned by small bands of men equipped with water and provisions to withstand a siege.

The Berber tribes warred incessantly among themselves. Blood feuds were frequent. If a man were killed his kinsmen were compelled to kill the slayer. In turn *his* relatives must avenge his death. This went on until nearly all the male members of a family had been exterminated. Often a man would sit in the tower of his house, rifle ready, waiting for a shot at his next-door neighbour; sometimes he would wait for days and weeks at a time.

The nomad Berbers dwell in tents woven from the hair of goats and camels, and carry their homes with them when leading their flocks and herds to other pastures. They have their summer and winter pastures, and spend their time travelling back and forth between them.

The oases scattered about the desert at irregular intervals vary in size, some being only large enough to shelter a family and its animals, others supporting a fluctuating population of anything up to fifty thousand people. Some contain a dozen or so villages and cover hundreds of square miles. Often these people supplemented their scanty livelihood by making raids on each other's cattle or on passing caravans. In the days when large caravans crossed the desert with loads of salt, gold dust, slaves, and ivory, this was a very profitable business, but the advance of European civilization has put an end to raiding and slave-trading.

The date-palm is the mainstay of life, and one can sometimes see hundreds or thousands of trees growing in an oasis. The date is an important article of trade, and it is an interesting sight at harvest-time to see boys run nimbly up the tree-trunks to cut off the clusters of red-gold fruit. After the coconut the date palm is the next interesting and useful member of the palm family. The trunk usually shoots up fifty or sixty feet without a branch, its summit crowned by a magnificent cluster of feather-shaped leaves. The dates grow in bunches weighing twenty to twenty-five pounds, and can be eaten fresh or dried. Cakes of dates pounded together form the principal food of the nomads when crossing the desert.

Most people imagine that an oasis consists of a patch of date-palms and a meagre water supply. In actual fact, as I have already pointed out, many of the oases cover a considerable area of ground, often thousands of acres, with a population also of thousands.

Though much of the surface of the Sahara is waterless, there are many indications of dried-up rivers. The surface streams seem to disappear into the sands, but actually find their outlet in underground pools which can be tapped by wells. In recent years the French have done a certain amount of boring for water and found it in considerable quantities at depths as great as four thousand feet. At El-Arfiane, between Tuggurt and Biskra, a new well produces 2,200 gallons of water a minute, while another, at Mraier, gives 88,000 gallons a minute. Unfortunately, it is not always possible to develop these new deep-water supplies, as the land in the oases belongs to a class of Arab landlords who let it out to individuals in small patches, to be cultivated on a sharing basis.

Sometimes a group of villages will have its own series of underground water-channels to tap the subterranean reservoirs and convey the water for considerable distances, often several miles, to the points where it is most needed. Many of these native water systems are of great antiquity, and represent a prodigious amount of labour.

The Berbers are an hospitable people, and if you are invited to dine in one of their camps or houses it is an entertaining affair.

Imagine a banquet in one of the big tents of a Berber chieftain, with brightly-coloured carpets on the floors and embroidered cushions for the guests to recline on. A slave brings soap, water, and towel for you to wash your right hand. "Blessed is the food eaten with the hand," says the Koran, and so no knives or forks are used, only the right hand. To use the left when eating is a breach of etiquette.

As you look out from under the rim of the tent at the surrounding desert, servants bring in dishes of roast meat and vegetables, which have been cooking outside in the open over a brushwood fire. The chieftain's sons wait upon the guest. The courses are many and varied ; as well as the main dish, there will be side-dishes consisting of strips of mutton served on wooden skewers, hard-boiled eggs, honey, nuts, almonds, and cakes of various kinds.

Later on a dish of *cous-cous*, a favourite Arab delicacy made of broken grains of wheat mixed with meat and vegetables, will be brought in. To eat *cous-cous* is a difficult art for a foreigner. The idea is to scoop up a little of the mixture in the fingers of the right hand, and twist it neatly into a ball ; but as it is hot and slippery, unless you have got the knack of doing it properly, you are more likely to drop it into your lap.

45

Every now and again the host, to mark his appreciation of his guest, will plunge a hand into the pot and pick out some delicacy which the guest must eat, whatever it may be, for a refusal would give great offence.

With the Berbers eating is regarded as a serious business, and nothing must be allowed to interfere with it. At long last everybody seems to be full, and slaves then bring water and towels again for you to wash your hands.

Finally, mint tea is served ; this is ordinary tea with mint leaves chopped up in it. It is sweet and hot, and not until you have drunk the three cups required by etiquette will you be allowed to depart.

So much for a Berber feast !

The Berber loves a festival, and particularly a wedding. Let me tell you of the wedding of a sultan's son, when barbaric splendour marked the marriage, with an Arabian Night's setting for wonderful festivities. It was a flashback to the old Berber days of golden glory, a revival of their once historic past, for which a large sum had been set aside. For this the sultan had adjusted his budget in accordance with the amounts given districts could supply, and successful candidates for posts were those who got the utmost out of the area committed to their charge.

The sultan's daughter-in-law was one of four lawful wives, as allowed by the Koran ; she was the daughter of the governor of Marrakesh. For two or three days Marrakesh was illuminated with candles, lamps, and lanterns, and on the wedding eve, the bride left her home for that of her future husband. She was enclosed in a box like a dovecote, placed on a richly caparisoned mule. The procession was headed by the chief priests of the mosque, with the friends and families of both parties.

An immense orchestra was distributed along the route. The town was on holiday and thousands of guests carried lamps of silver, brass, copper, and coloured paper, while luminous fountains in every square shot forth vari-coloured water.

As the bride left her father's home, all the lights in the house were extinguished, as a sign that the light of love and beauty had left for ever.

Arriving at the home of her future husband, she was taken to her rooms, where the final touches were put to her complexion, her feet were re-covered with henna, and a dish of the national *cous-cous* was placed before her by the mother-in-law. Apparently etiquette demanded that she eat only a morsel, but must put a little on her nose and wish herself luck. The bridegroom then took over the lady, still veiled, and served up more of the *cous-cous*, which she ate.

Following this came the unveiling, when the husband would get a view of her for the first time in his life. It was possibly comforting for him to reflect that he still had three more chances !

Two days later the dovecote was placed on the roof, as a signal that she was " At Home " to her women friends. A reception followed, and high jinks went on for some days ; everyone gave dinners to everyone else, and every variety of Berber dish was served ; alms were distributed to the beggars, the poor were regaled, and tea, flavoured with mint and verbena, was dispensed.

Unlike the Tuaregs, the Berbers like dancing, and the dancing-girls are regarded with special favour. The presents at this marriage included everything from bracelets, anklets, and gold ornaments, precious stones, brocades, and rolls of silk, down to the humble bag of almond nuts from the Berber shepherd.

I ought now to say something about the head of the Berbers, who is the Sultan of Morocco, of holy descent, deriving his prestige and authority from a connection with the Prophet. Time has invested the Sultan with much sanctity, magnified by years of tradition, and with all the air of romance and mystery. He is the living representative of the soul of the Berbers, and pre-eminent above all his subjects as the highest spiritual authority. He can do anything his fancy may dictate. The French, however, with tact and discretion, see to it that the Sultan does not overstep the mark.

When the ruler goes out he is clothed in flowing white robes, mounted on a white horse, with a pale green silken saddle and stirrups of gold. Alongside walks a Nubian bearing a gigantic red parasol as protection, while another waves a cloth of purest linen to keep the flies away. A band of musicians, each clothed in white robes, accompanies him.

The Sultan is a patron of the arts and sometimes visits the Karaouin mosque, sacred seat of learning. Here the doctors and scribes of the faith are taught. It is a vast place and can hold twenty thousand; its long corridors echo with the chant of prayer and the muezzins intoning to Allah; its passages and courtyards laid with mosaic glimmer in the sun, and there is a sense of proportion and dignified design. Graceful columns support Saracenic arches with vaulted roofs; through the tinted windows comes cream-coloured light; beyond are waving palms.

Here the Sultan comes to pray; and when he has shared with his subjects the call of the muezzin, he returns, slowly and majestically, to his palace in the Arabian Nights city of Fez, or Marrakesh, or wherever it may be.

Those who study at the Karaouin Mosque are honoured men, and the student-traveller moves about the country at a minimum of expense and a maximum of luxury.

After midday prayers the bazaars and streets are crowded. Shopping is easy, for the jewellers and silversmiths are in one street, the potters in another, and cloth, brocades, shoes, saddlery, swords, hardware and leather, each in its own domain. The shops are like kennels, open to front and sides, and the shopkeeper sits among his wares with an air of complete indifference. In fact, he hardly deigns to notice the customer.

Women in their long gowns and hoods, with two round holes for the eyes, pass to and fro.

Streets are irregular and frequently not more than four or five feet wide, running in and out and leading in every direction. Houses lean drunkenly, shutting out the sun. After sunset it is pitch dark, the night air emphasizing the smell from the open drains.

Here and there are the fortune-tellers and sorcerers. They gather the credulous crowd and for a halfpenny or so deal out lifelong prosperity to their clients. Here also is the professional letter-writer, an institution in all Berber towns and villages. He sits cross-legged with pen and paper spread out upon his knees; clients gather round and narrate the text of documents, petitions, and letters, and the scribe commits it all to paper. Education being poor, the professional amanuensis comes into his own on

Portrait of a Berber.

A desert mother tends her child in its
hanging, home-made crib.

market days when the terms of a bargain have to be recorded and deeds of sale drawn up.

There are schools in most towns, though the mosque is usually the seat of learning. With the exception of reading and writing and the dogmatic teaching of the Koran, practically nothing is learned, for the instructors themselves are in need of education and it is really a case of the blind leading the blind. The pupils sit on the ground, or, at the more pretentious schools, on wooden forms, with desks made from logs. They sing whatever is set for study, for the Berbers have the fixed idea that the mind absorbs knowledge through the ears rather than the eyes.

The Kabyles are another branch of the Berber race, all of whom are known under the general name of Moors.

The Kabyle was largely responsible for the capture of North Africa for Islam; they are of fighting stock, star-gazers and mathematical materialists, whose holy capital at Fez, where the lamps hang low in the mosques and the high walls ambuscade the streets, gave its civic freedom to but one Christian—Marshal Lyautey.

The French first came to the Sahara when they invaded Algeria in 1830 to overthrow the Barbary corsairs. The enemy, who numbered many Kabyles in their ranks, put up a great fight, their general being one Ben Aissa, who drove back the first French force. It required a second expedition to restore authority.

So well did the Kabyles fight that the second expedition was partly formed of these irregulars, who were destined to become famous in the annals of French warfare. They were known as the Zouaves, wearing a distinctive dress which was the fore-runner of the Zouave uniform so familiar in the French army, the red fez, short close-fitting jacket, and big, baggy, red trousers. The French realized that here was first-rate material, and they set to work to make the most of it, enlisting these Kabyles in special regiments and using them as shock troops. They soon acquired a reputation for their brilliant conduct in the field, their dash in attack, and the reliance that could be placed on them in moments of danger. They become a *corps d'élite*, but, unfortunately, in later years they lost the national character; there were insufficient

Kabyles to keep them up to strength. These warlike people were like the Swiss, the Hessians, and Hanoverians ; they hired themselves out as mercenary soldiers and enjoyed the fighting as a picnic. Once it was over they lost their enthusiasm : peace-time barrack life does not suit the Kabyle ; and so they went streaming back to the desert and the villages to await another campaign.

To maintain the original regiments, at any rate in name, adventurous spirits were enrolled from all over Europe, and the old-time allure died away.

Although they were semi-barbaric, with no knowledge of modern warfare, they adopted the tactics that suited their own country and the Kabyle mode of fighting. These Zouaves made the best use of cover, were expert shots with their long-barrelled guns, and when they got to close quarters used them as clubs. Like the Pathans of the Indian frontier they were swift of foot and could march thirty or forty miles a day with ease. The heat and dust were nothing to these wiry people, and they held firmly to the belief that should they be killed in battle all the joys of paradise would be theirs. As fighters the Kabyles were a real and living interest, worthy of study on the spot, but their spirit could only be assimilated by close contact and by moving with them in the desert.

Lyautey understood the Kabyle as few men have done. Like the famous John Nicholson of Indian Mutiny fame, he fought them with their own weapons and psychology. Perhaps he had taken a leaf out of Nicholson's book.

They are tall, strong, and stately, and train into fine cavalry. Those who take to trade do so with one ambition, to raise enough money to buy a plot of land in their own village. Their language is known as " Zouave ". As followers of the Sunni sect of Mahommedanism they have a fanatical faith in Mohammed and the power of the curved scimitar of Islam.

As of the Berbers, the Sultan of Morocco is liege lord of the Kabyles, and they pay tribute in kind, consisting, *inter alia*, of presents of Kabyle girls. The Kabyles, when born, are as white as English children, but exposure to the sun gradually turns them dark. Kabyle girls, however, remain white, being, like other women of the harem, protected from light. So they preserve their whiteness and beauty, statuesque blue-eyed brunettes of the world. By their blue eyes, this Hamitic race is thus distinguished by a distinctly Nordic feature.

Women in the harem live in privacy. No man, except the husband, must ever approach the threshold, and the husband always eats alone. Personal service is provided by the women of the bath, of the soap, of the dishes, of the tea, and those of the goblet who pour out his drinks ; so the wives are free to devote themselves to retaining the man's affection.

The senior mother-in-law rules among the women, who spend much time on make-up, for they are no believers in beauty unadorned. Paint and powder are freely used, as well as a henna dye to defeat grey hairs and to give the red tint that is a hall-mark of beauty.

Who shall be the most beautiful and captivating ? Who shall wear the finest silks and satins ? Rivalry breeds conspiracy and intrigue, one endeavouring to profit at the expense of another, or to create a vacancy in a household to be filled by a friend or relative.

Bribery is common in wealthy Kabyle homes, and an applicant for favours is successful in proportion to the amount of silver dust cast in the path of those in authority. The penalty of unfaithfulness, or misconduct in any form, is often drastic, and the privilege of punishment is not ignored by the husband. One of these chiefs, on learning that I was unmarried, said to me one day, " How strange it must be for you not to have any women to beat ! "

All kinds of things happen in a harem. Poison is often administered, for here is a land where no law controls the sale of drugs and potions. A certificate of the cause of death is unknown.

The Koran lays down that a Moslem shall have only four wives, but there is no limit to the number of concubines. When a sheikh or high official dies, his widows may find homes amongst the merchant and trading classes, who by such marriages acquire not only reflected glory, but a certain amount of jewellery and money.

As we have seen, the Kabyles and their fellow-Moors carried the Crescent through Spain up into France, and to-day they are just as rigid followers of the Prophet as their ancestors were centuries before them. This was evident to me during a visit which happened to coincide with the feast of Ramazan. This is the greatest religious observance of the Moslem faith and one that directly affects two hundred million Moslems. It is incumbent on all to observe the fast, which lasts thirty days, a duty of such importance that Mohammed characterized it as the gate of religion.

There are twelve months in the Moslem calendar, alternatively of thirty and twenty-nine days ; the advent of Ramazan, therefore, varies, for the Moslem year being lunar, each month runs through the various seasons in the course of thirty-two solar years. The reason for the choice of Ramazan for the period of fasting is that the Koran is said to have come down from Heaven in that month.

During the fast no food whatever must be taken between dawn and nightfall. The fast is rendered null and void even if perfumes are inhaled. There can be no form of material pleasure. There must be no bathing, nor is the true believer permitted to swallow his own saliva. The orthodox Moslem will not open his mouth for fear of breathing more air than is essential.

During darkness, eating and drinking are permitted. No particle of food must be left in the mouth, for even a grain of rice in the teeth is sufficient to destroy the fast, and the reward to be gained in the hereafter decreases proportionately. A Moslem now must not touch a woman, and to kiss her is disastrous.

While the rich may withstand the fast by turning night into day, its rigours fall heavily on the poor and industrial classes, who must continue their daily work, and when the month of Ramazan occurs during the summer with its eighteen hours of daylight, fortitude and physical fitness are demanded. Nevertheless, when the famous Orientalist, Sir Richard Burton, who spoke twenty-nine languages fluently and had a nodding acquaintance with forty-eight more, was living in Alexandria disguised as an Arab doctor, he found his patients refused to break the fast, even when they knew that such an attitude meant death.

At the end of the thirty days the fast ends, and revels and junketings take place, this period of joy being known as the "feast of the breaking of the fast". The reaction takes every form of conviviality, festive song and dance, the wearing of light attire and brilliant jewellery, and the distributing of presents.

We have seen how the Berbers and the Kabyles live and have their being, and now I might make a brief mention of the flora and fauna of the Sahara.

The trees are the date-palm, acacia, evergreen, and a kind of willow. The date-palm is the mainstay of life; it grows in hundreds and sometimes thousands at the oases, and its fruit is an important article of trade. Acacias are found in limited numbers along the banks of dried-up rivers. They supply the camel with food from their small, thorny branches.

There is no accounting for a camel's taste, for he also eats the abisgee, a green and willowy tree with a smell that reminds one of the cats' house at the Zoo.

Birds of all kinds flourish in the Sahara; larks soaring up from the oases, and warblers and finches, escaping the European winters. Sand grouse are there, and make as good eating as their Scottish relations. The voice of the ring-dove and the turtle-dove is heard in the desert, with its soothing and sometimes melancholy influence. The cuckoo stays for a brief spell on his way to Central Africa, although he is said never to "cuckoo", keeping that for Europe only. There are martins, swallows, and swifts, as well as blue rock-pigeons, but most of the birds are migratory and come to the desert only when it is at its best.

It is splendid to see such a variety of plumage flitting about among plants that, despite lack of water, show great flower vitality, although for years they have not had a drink. Nature has, however, fortified them to withstand this thirst. One such plant is the rose of Jericho—as lovely as a Maréchal Niel, and with as fine a scent.

THE MAN IN THE RED TUNIC

I HAVE no space to record the wonders of all the various Saharan oases, for they need a book to themselves, so I have chosen to tell something of one of the most important and fascinating of them—Tafilelt. This great oasis lies south of the Great Atlas Mountains of Morocco, and controls the caravan route from the Niger to Tangier. Formerly it was a separate kingdom, and Sijjilmassa, its capital, was one of the great cities of North Africa, with a population of over a quarter-of-a-million people.

For hundreds of years Tafilelt was known to Europeans only by hearsay, the oasis being extremely difficult of access. It was holy ground, for there in a closely-guarded sanctuary lay the bones of *Mulai* (My Lord) Reshed, the conqueror of Morocco. He led his cohorts over the Atlas Mountains three hundred years ago, and founded the dynasty that survives to-day. Tafilelt was also a land of exile. It was the custom of the Moorish sultans to dispatch thither their surplus sons, who, being shereefs or descendants of the Prophet Mohammed, fanatically repulsed any attempts by Europeans to reach the oasis.

But reach it they eventually did. First to describe it was René Caillié, that dauntless son of a French shoemaker, returning from his amazing journey across the Sahara from Timbuktu. That was in 1828. Tafilelt remained undisturbed until the arrival of Gerhard Rohlfs in 1864. These first explorers looked in vain for the buildings of fabled Sijjilmassa. The city was gone, destroyed by fire and sword, and only ruins remained. The first Englishman arrived in 1894, when Walter Harris of *The Times* travelled there in disguise from Marrakesh.

Then came the French and the beginnings of the pacification of the Sahara. French troops fought their way over the Atlas Mountains and established themselves in Tafilelt. But the fighting men of the Sahara were in no mood to yield lightly. They rose and drove out the white men and destroyed their fort. The French retired to the River Ziz, and built there a new walled town called Erfoud.

All this happened during the closing years of the First World War, when the French had other things to think about than Saharan conquest. Not till 1932 did they return to Tafilelt, rebuild their fortress, and press on into the Sahara. Tafilelt was now open to the world, or at least to those fortunate individuals who could secure permission from the French military authorities to visit it.

The history of Tafilelt is the history of many another Saharan oasis. I have not chosen it for these reasons, however, but because it is associated with a romantic name connected with the conquest of the Northern Sahara—Henri de Bournazel.

Wherever you travel in Morocco or the northern Sahara you will hear stories of de Bournazel, for he is now almost a legendary figure. His dauntless courage and the scarlet tunic which he always wore won for him, from friends and foes alike, the title of the " Red Man ". So much did he seem to have a charmed life, so often did death by sword or bullet pass him by, that he became known as " the man they could not kill ". He rose from the rank of trooper to become governor of those little-known lands south of the Great Atlas Mountains, whose savage tribesmen were only finally conquered in 1934.

Even to-day, if you should speak, as I have done, to men who worked and fought alongside the " Red Man " during those exciting days, you will see their eyes light up at the mention of his name, and they will immediately launch into tales of his courage and audacity, tales no less incredible because they happen to be true. But his finest memorial is the peaceful, prosperous countryside which he helped to create, with its growing towns and villages, its fertile fields and date forests.

" De Bournazel, *monsieur* ?—ah, there was a man for you ! " Such was the remark made by a French officer. " A man as brave as a lion, yet as clever as a fox. It did you good to meet him. Maybe you have heard the tale of how, during the war against Abdel Krim, the rebel leader of the Riff tribes-men, de Bournazel went to the relief of a besieged chieftain with only a hundred men. Listen !

" There should have come reinforcements, but they did not

arrive, and his party was surrounded by Abdel Krim's brigands. He started to fight his way back to the nearest French post, but his men deserted, and soon there were only about fifty left. These scoundrels told him they would not fight any more, that they would lay down their arms. Why be killed when it was hopeless to fight? The Red Man laughed at them, took his riding-whip and revolver, and told them to run back home : he would fight the Riffs alone. Then he walked forward single-handed to meet the rebel tribesmen.

"These savages would have taken him alive, to kill him slowly by torture ; but suddenly his men came charging up from behind and drove the Riffs back. His bravery and contempt had shamed them into coming to his rescue. Such was the stuff of which de Bournazel was made."

The "Red Man" started his military career in the ranks, though he was the son of a general and came from an old aristocratic French family. He joined the cavalry at the age of eighteen, and a year later was mentioned in dispatches at the Battle of the Marne. He was then a subaltern, eager for more fighting, and the end of the war was a disappointment for him.

It was in North Africa, however, that he was destined to achieve lasting fame ; a country in the process of being conquered was the obvious destination for a man of his temperament. These were the years when Abdel Krim, the great Berber chieftain, was at the height of his career. He almost broke the power of Spain in Africa, and came near to reconquering Morocco from the French. De Bournazel joined the Spahis, or native cavalry, when he arrived in Africa in 1921, and during the next five years had enough fighting to satisfy even his fire-eating spirit.

An incident which occurred in May, 1925, is typical of the man. He then commanded a band of Goums, or native irregular cavalry, and had been given the task of guarding a mobile column of French troops. De Bournazel interpreted this to mean that he could conduct a private war against the Berbers. At the head of his men, his brilliant red tunic ever in the front, he charged a strongly held enemy position and had captured the place almost before the enemy realized what was happening. It was thus that he gained the title of *Bou Vesta Hamra*—" The Man

Among the pillars and arches of the Great
Mosque at Karaouin.

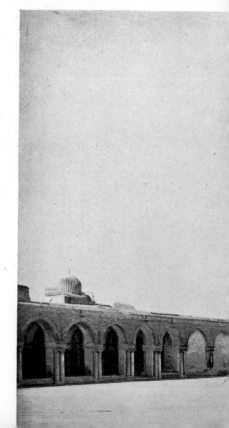

The minaret from which the muezzin calls the faithful to prayer.

The court and cloisters of the Karaouin; Mosque, Morocco's sacred seat of learning.

This pulpit in the Great Mosque at Karaouin
is of carved wood.

in the Red Tunic ". Abdel Krim offered a reward of a quarter-of-a-million francs for his body, dead or alive.

On another occasion, when the conquest of the northern Sahara was in progress in 1931, a violent sand-storm completely disorganized the French forces. De Bournazel kept his cavalry together, and, without waiting for reinforcements, attacked the enemy and defeated them. He had been ordered by his commanding officer not to wear his red tunic, which made him a target for the enemy's fire, but to wear khaki instead. He obeyed, and was machine-gunned by a French aeroplane which mistook him for a Berber chieftain. After that he vowed that never again would he fight without wearing his famous red coat.

De Bournazel spent the five years after the surrender of Abdel Krim in 1926, in France, living the life of an ordinary French gentleman. But restless spirits such as his cannot settle down easily to the life of ordinary people. He missed the excitements of Africa.

Though northern Morocco was pacified, the desert country south of the Great Atlas Mountains still remained unconquered. Out in the Sahara lay the great oasis of Tafilelt, ruled by Berber chieftains and tribesmen who for over thirteen years had defied the power of France.

In 1931 the French Government finally decided to complete the conquest of the north-western Sahara ; and when the Red Man heard that an army was being formed for this purpose, he promptly volunteered to command a group of native cavalry. At once he was sent by Colonel—later General—Giraud to the desert city of Erfoud, to prepare a way for the French troops.

What was this land, for possession of which French and Berbers were presently to fight so savagely ? If you look at the map you will see that Morocco consists of two distinct regions. The northern half was completely pacified after the First World War : this is the new Morocco created by the French, with its fine roads, hotels, schools, and towns, where the tourist can travel in perfect safety. But south of the Atlas Mountains lay the " Zone of Insecurity ", the stronghold of the Berber diehards, whose conquest was not completed until 1934. Here a Christian was still liable to be killed on the spot, to the greater glory of Allah.

When I travelled there later on, the curfew was still sounded nightly at sundown, and riflemen patrolled the barbed-wire barricades drawn across the roads. Despite these precautions, a dare-devil raider, Zait ou Mohammed, got through the barricades at Tinerhir Post one evening and shot dead three of the French Foreign Legion who were drinking at the bar. It was two months before he was finally tracked down and killed after a battle in which machine-guns and hand-grenades had to be used.

This was the land and the sort of people which France planned to add to her empire in 1931. Tafilelt oasis was occupied in 1932, after being attacked simultaneously by artillery, tanks, cavalry, and bombing planes ; but Belgacem N'Gadi, the Berber leader, escaped through the French lines to carry on the fight in the Atlas Mountains.

De Bournazel was made governor of Tafilelt, where he proved himself to be not only a fighting-man, but a brilliant administrator as well. He started irrigation schemes, built roads, houses, hospitals, fed the poor, and gradually restored the prosperity of the region. For the first time in centuries travellers could pass freely through the northern Sahara.

The Berber diehards still held out in two regions, on the Djebel Baddou and the Djebel Sagho. On the summit of the latter mountain a group of eight hundred tribesmen made their last stand. It was a natural fortress of caves, rocks, and galleries. They were bombarded by aircraft and artillery for five days, and then the French forces moved in to take the place by storm. But the Berbers were still full of fight, and a hail of bullets met the French troops.

Attack after attack was launched, the French doggedly fighting their way up the mountain foot by foot. Men on either side died like flies, the mountain top resounded to the crash of bombs and gunfire, while the burning African sun blazed down relentlessly. It was the hardest and most violent campaign in all the history of the conquest of Morocco.

The French forces at last reached an open space just below the summit, and prepared for the final assault. De Bournazel had been ordered to wear a grey cloak over his red tunic to lessen the risk of his being hit. Grumbling, he obeyed, for he believed that it was bad luck for him to hide his red tunic.

The attack began. A few minutes later he went down with a bullet in his stomach. He rose, and still clutching his riding-whip and revolver, continued the climb. In that storm of flame and steel, men were falling fast, and at last his own men turned and fled. He threw his empty revolver at them contemptuously and went on alone. A second bullet struck him and he fell, never to rise again.

Two men dragged him behind a rock, and there, on February 28, 1933, on a windswept mountain-top amid a storm of bullets, died Henri de Bournazel.

There were no more direct attacks. General Giraud decided to starve the Berbers into submission. For a month the long-range guns sent shells crashing into the mountain-top, killing men, women, and children, and destroying the wells which were the only water supply. Only when death by thirst faced them did Hasso ou Ba Slam, the Berber chieftain, come down the mountain with a white flag to surrender.

To-day the traveller who scans the grey summit of the mountain will learn that it has a new name—Mount Bournazel.

A few months later the tribesmen on Djebel Baddou also surrendered, and the only Berbers who remained unconquered were the savage Blue Moors who inhabited the sandy wastes of Rio de Oro and Mauretania.

Strange lands, these, and strange people!

§

THE BLUE MOORS

IF you were asked to point out on a map one of the least-known lands in the world you would probably point to the jungles of the Amazon or perhaps the frozen deserts round the North or South Poles. But there is an unknown land much closer to us than this, for just south of Morocco is the great stretch of desert known vaguely as Rio de Oro, or the Spanish Sahara, which is one of the largest unexplored areas in the world. It stretches almost without a break to the River Senegal, is practically unknown to Europeans, and is inhabited by some of the most savage nomads on earth. Seeing that death or slavery awaits anyone attempting to penetrate this well-nigh inaccessible region, it may rightly be termed a " forbidden land ".

The pilots of the Campagnie Général Aéropostale have many stories to tell of this wild land. They have to fly over it to reach Villa Cisneros, the jumping-off place for South America. A pilot engaged on the pioneer postal service between Morocco and South America said that if an aeroplane were forced down in the desert the pilots were promptly taken prisoner by the Berbers, who either killed them outright or held them to ransom.

" They are a bloodthirsty lot, those Blue Moors ! " he declared. " Many of our pilots have come down in that God-forsaken land and have been captured. Luckily airmen are usually kept alive and ransomed."

He told how Pilot Gourp and two passengers had been captured in Rio de Oro ; one man had been killed outright, and Gourp himself badly wounded. Two other airmen, Erabe and Pintado, had been killed ; their companion had been tortured, tied to a camel, and then sent off, bleeding from many wounds, in the general direction of Agadir.

It is curious that such a state of affairs can exist in the twentieth century. How is it that the Spanish Sahara has not been efficiently pacified ? Existing political conditions are the result of international jealousies. The region is nominally under Spanish sovereignty, but Spain is not strong enough to conquer the warlike tribes of the desert, her rule being confined to two small settlements on the coast. The tribesmen remain independent and hostile to white men, but since the territory is Spanish, no other nation can send troops to subdue them.

Rio de Oro stretches roughly from the River Dra to Cape Blanco, is some six hundred miles long by two hundred miles wide, and is mostly covered by sand and steppe. It seems to be the only African territory of any size which has never been crossed by a white man, and almost nothing is known about it ; for nearly a hundred years no explorer had penetrated the interior. The inhabitants, the Blue Moors, still live in the style of the tenth century, ruled by powerful chieftains and hereditary saints.

What little knowledge we have of the country comes from the accounts of the few people who have managed to visit portions of it. The first is believed to have been Leopold Panet, a Senegalese mulatto, who in 1850 travelled across Rio de Oro on his way from Senegal to Morocco. He was disguised as a Moslem, and journeyed with a caravan bound for Smara, a desert city in the interior. Before reaching that place, Panet was attacked and robbed by his companions. He was wounded, but managed to get to Mogador, where he died.

In 1887 Camille Douls, a French explorer, landed on the western coast near Cape Garnet and set out on foot for Smara. Captured by the Berbers, he was promptly sentenced to death, and buried up to his neck in the sand. Undaunted, however, he began to chant verses from the Koran, whereupon his captors decided that he must be a Moslem, and dug him up again. They allowed him to travel with them into the interior, and he spent five months wandering through the eastern sand desert.

At last he reached the dried-up river valley known as Sequiet el Hamara, in which Smara is situated. He then went on to the desert city of Tindouf and became formally engaged to marry a Berber girl. On the pretext of obtaining money for her dowry he escaped into Morocco, where he was killed by the Arabs a year later.

Travellers to Tisnit in South Morocco often encounter the Blue Moors there, for it is the most northerly market frequented by the nomads. I remember my first sight of them. Out of the distance approached a line of camels, ridden by men clothed in robes of indigo blue, with veils over their faces so that only their eyes were visible. These were the mysterious " Blue Men " from the strange regions to the south.

They are not Moors, of course, but Berbers, kinsmen of the fierce Tuareg of the central Sahara. Like the Tuareg the men go veiled, not as a matter of tribal law, but merely as a protection against the swirling desert sand. There has been little influx of Arab blood among them, so the Berber stock has remained relatively pure. Like all Berbers they are brave and cruel, ready to fight on the slightest provocation. Their main occupation seems to be tending their herds, and raiding villages and caravans. They are not fanatically religious, having discarded many orthodox Mohammedan beliefs on the plea of being nomads; they allow their women to go unveiled, and do not observe the fast of Ramazan.

Smara was another of those secret cities of the Sahara about which many stories gathered during the course of the years. It was said to be a wealthy place, standing far out in the heart of a black desert, guarded by two strong castles, and inhabited by fanatical Blue Moors. It was believed that no European had ever visited this mysterious place, and that all explorers who had tried to reach it had either been turned back, or had not returned at all.

Just as the story of Timbuktu acquainted us with the efforts of that remarkable man, René Caillié, so the story of Smara introduces us to another equally brave and determined explorer who was willing to give his life to the solving of the secrets of the Sahara. His name was Michel Vieuchange.

To explore the unknown western Sahara—that had been Vieuchange's ambition since boyhood. To reach a forbidden city, Smara, in its black desert, to be the first Christian there— what greater thrill could a man have? It was a hundred years since Caillié's amazing journey, and the nomads of the desert were as savage and inhospitable as ever. The twentieth century stopped at the southern boundary of Morocco. Once a man passed beyond that, he would take his life in his hands, and find himself in a region where tenth-century modes of life and thought prevailed. But it would be worth it.

Vieuchange waited, collecting all the information about the people of the Spanish Sahara. One day came electrifying news— French airmen had flown over Smara and brought back the first news of its appearance. There was no time to waste if he was to be first to reach the city; it was time to go.

This was not the early nineteenth century; this was the twentieth: Vieuchange started off on September 10, 1930. He had planned the journey for over a year, and left the Wad Massa, twenty miles north of Tisnit, travelling with a party of Berber nomads. He knew his life would be forfeit if his identity were discovered, but he was determined to be the first white man to set foot in Smara.

He could speak but little Arabic or Berber, so it was arranged that he should travel disguised as a woman. Accordingly he was muffled up in a large blue *haik*, or cloak, and veil, which gave him the necessary cover for making notes. His equipment consisted of two watches, two compasses, two cameras, and sundry medicines for dysentery, malaria, and snake-bite. He hoped to reach Smara in twelve or fourteen days.

At first, in order to allay the suspicions of the border tribesmen, Vieuchange had to trudge along on foot with the other women. Afterwards he was permitted to ride on a donkey. The first day, they crossed the stony desert to Tisnit, camping for the night outside the walls. Here Vieuchange was able to shave and stain his skin dark brown with permanganate of potash.

Three days later they reached the territory of the fierce Kaid Madani, in a region hostile to the French. Vieuchange had many difficulties to contend with ; he suffered from the cold at night, from blistered feet, and lack of sleep. He had to learn to behave like a Berber woman, and to remember many little points, such as curling up like a dog when he slept, and never on his back—that would have indicated that he was a Jewess.

The party passed little walled towns, where the men were armed with Lebel rifles and bayonets. They crossed rocky mountains, where the traveller must always be on guard against attack. Sometimes they had difficulty with the chiefs of the various territories they entered, who demanded toll before allowing them to proceed on their way.

Finally they reached the town of Tigilit, in the centre of a small oasis which produced dates and maize. One night a hundred desert raiders stormed the place, killed most of the men, and drove off all the camels and goats. Owing to this mishap, Vieuchange and his party had to stay there for a fortnight until they could secure fresh mounts.

On October 4 the explorer crossed the River Dra. He was now travelling with two sheikhs, one of whom was overlord of three thousand tribesmen. At this point things began to go wrong. Their guide collapsed with a poisoned foot ; then they encountered another band of desert raiders, who compelled them to retreat to Tigilit. So Vieuchange's first attempt at reaching Smara ended in failure.

Nothing daunted, he immediately planned a second expedition, but fifteen days passed before he could set out. Crossing the Djebel Ouargziz, he traversed the Dra again. As I saw it from the airship, this desert river is usually dry, with only scattered pools of water during the rainy season. Beyond the Dra was a black pebbly desert where Vieuchange was able to ride on a camel.

But this luxury was short-lived, for soon afterwards the little party came upon the tracks of several thousand riders. Fearful that he might be discovered, Vieuchange's guides hid him in a wicker hamper on the back of a donkey. This was sheer torture, for he had to lie doubled up, unable to move hand or foot, and tormented by heat, dust, and flies. Such was the Frenchman's determination, however, that he endured this agonizing form of locomotion.

They entered the yellow desert of Ga'a, which is flat and devoid of vegetation. It took them two days to cross this waterless region. Then came a black stony area, on the further edge of which was pitched a camp of three thousand tents. Here they encountered a party of Blue Moors bound for Smara, and again Vieuchange had to be hidden in the wicker hamper.

At long last, after crossing numerous deserts, the explorer saw before him the goal he had come so far to seek—Smara, the forbidden city.

The town possessed two *kasbahs,* or castles, a mosque, a few flat-roofed houses inhabited by wealthy tribesmen, sundry market buildings, and numerous nomad tents. There were no encircling walls. The houses rose straight out of the flat desert, grouped round the castles and the mosque.

Vieuchange found Smara to be practically dead. Like Timbuktu, Sijjilmassa, and other noted Saharan centres, it is now a crumbling and well-nigh deserted town, awakening to a semblance of life only when various caravans meet there to dispose of slaves and arms, making use of the place because the massive old buildings offer a certain amount of shelter from raiders.

Vieuchange was able to spend a few hours exploring the town, then he was hurried away by his anxious guides. Before

A Tuareg—" Lord of the Desert ".

Legionaries—Guardians of the Sahara.

leaving, however, he wrote a brief record of his journey, placed it in a bottle, and buried it under the floor of one of the castles, as proof that he had actually been there.

The march back to the Dra was a nightmare. Many camels died, some of his men deserted, and he himself was half-dead with dysentery. When they approached the sphere of French influence, his companions, fearing that they were going to lose the money he had promised them, threatened to kill him. He was able to pacify them, but by the time they reached the frontier city of Tiznit he was a dying man. An aeroplane took him to Agadir, where, four days later, on November 30, 1930, the brave explorer died. Another episode in the history of the Sahara was ended.

§

THE PEOPLE OF THE VEIL

IN this sinister and mystic land the Tuaregs—the People of the Veil—very little known to the outer world, are the overlords, the Knights of the Desert, whose home is under the blue sky, for they will not stay beneath a permanent roof, regarding it as ill-luck. They shun the world in general ; they consider the desert as their own and dislike the sight of other men. No one knows exactly whence they came ; they are so difficult of approach and hold themselves so much aloof that they are called by other tribes the " Abandoned of God ". They are physically, however, a magnificent race of people, and live by raiding—a battle-loving, plunder-hungry tribe who, as predatory and untameable raiders, are as bad as can be found anywhere. For ages it has been their custom to go pillaging and killing in the lands adjacent to the Sahara. These things constitute their prime occupation, their business, and their sport.

To reach the Tuareg country you travel a thousand miles due south from Algiers. Here, at an altitude of a mile, surrounded on every side by the mighty peaks of the Ahaggar mountains, whose crimson sides are streaked with snow, stands Fort Laperrine ; Tamanrasset is its Berber name. This red fort, with its crenellated walls, is garrisoned by fifty Tuaregs, who have overcome their aversion to foreigners to the extent of serving as soldiers of France.

Beyond the fort, under the shadow of a nine-thousand-foot mountain, stands the camp of the Amenokal, or Sultan of the Tuaregs. On approaching the tents you are surrounded by a swarm of men in dark-purple, flowing robes, with turbans and blue veils. They make an impressive picture, armed as they are with slender steel spears, long, straight swords, and big camel-hide shields.

The Tuaregs are the most mobile raiders on earth. Gigantic, silent people, they are mounted on camels trained to rise silently, and move off immediately at a fast pace, unlike the ordinary camel—a noisy beast that resents the order to get up and move on.

The Tuareg looks the typical raider when you see him in the dusk suddenly bearing down on your camp, veiled to the eyes and giving the appearance of a ghostly monk of the Inquisition. A sword hangs at his side, and a rifle is slung over one shoulder. He comes so quietly, and looks so huge silhouetted against the horizon, that it forms a mental picture not easily forgotten.

The Tuareg is a Moslem ; but totally unlike any other follower of the Prophet. Religion is by no means a passion with him, and I doubt if a Tuareg has ever made the pilgrimage to Mecca. These giant men are a law unto themselves ; they can be friendly and smiling, and they can be fickle and treacherous as well. They observe so few Moslem customs that the Arabs regard them as savages. There are traditions of an earlier religion among them, possibly Christianity, as evinced by the use of the cross among their ornaments. Their straight Crusader-like swords may also indicate a former Christian heritage. They are the only Berbers to have evolved a form of writing, but their history is forgotten.

The Tuareg is no tiller of the soil—there is little to till ; in fact, he disdains all work and devotes himself to the pastime of war. The Tuaregs have a proverb : " Shame enters the family that tills the soil."

The remarkable feature about these people is the veil, worn in all other Moslem countries by the women, but here adopted solely by the men. How the custom arose none can say—not even the Tuaregs themselves. Perhaps in ages long past it began from a desire to protect themselves from the rays of the sun and the whirling sand of the desert. At all events, the Tuareg would consider himself steeped in shame were he to uncover. He never takes off the veil in the presence of others, and even his nearest relative cannot look upon his face. He does not even remove it when he goes to sleep. These children of the desert take to the veil when they are about fourteen years of age, and from then onwards it is an inseparable part of their lives.

From that age, too, the training of the Tuareg commences, with all its intensity and severe ritual. He must fit himself for the game of war and raiding, the only item in his education, a trial that resolves itself into a case of the survival of the fittest. He must be able to go without water for four or five days in a land where it is scarce, and found only at intervals, often of two hundred miles and more, and to exist without food for an even longer period, and still keep fit and ready for the fray.

Sometimes in the desert the Tuareg's camel may sicken and die, but the veiled rider goes on afoot, and has been known to cover as much as two hundred miles in a couple of days. It is this tremendous physical endurance, this ability to go for long distances without food and water, that has inspired in all other tribes adjacent to the Tuareg country such a superstitious dread.

The Tuaregs when they start on a raid do it to a preconceived plan. They cover an area perhaps as large as France, and in their operations gather a great deal into the net, men, women, and children, livestock, and portable goods. There is, however, method in the Tuareg madness ; they leave a certain number of inhabitants in each settlement, for next year, or the year after, the raid may be repeated and the intervening period gives time for goods, animate and inanimate, to accumulate !

They have many curious manners and customs, and rigid rules covering the game of war. When on a raid no self-respecting Tuareg would steal another man's wife ; it is an unpardonable sin and punished with the utmost severity.

I heard of a case that met with drastic treatment. A raiding party had attacked a Tuareg camp, for there are opposing factions, and when not engaged in fighting a common enemy they fight and raid among themselves. The young and pretty wife of a man in the enemy's camp had been carried off, in defiance of time-honoured tradition, by which the life of the Tuareg is regulated. Instant and relentless action had to be taken, so the avengers set out on the warpath. The return raid was swift and sudden; it came at dawn, with the rush of those spectral figures in an overwhelming attack, the cutting down of some of them, and the capture of the offender who had so outraged the standard of Tuareg honour. The Sahara has ants of a large and voracious breed, and so the culprit was buried up to his neck in a hole in the sand adjacent to an ant-hill, which was then broken open so that the ants might swarm out and seek their living food. The next morning nothing but a clean white skull remained above the yellow sand; the Tuareg wife-stealer had paid the penalty of his crime.

There is great respect shown to women; in fact, in many ways a woman is more important than a man; for, as already remarked, she goes entirely unveiled; she can divorce her husband when she feels inclined; she proposes to the man of her choice; and the Tuareg girl travels long distances to see her fiancé. No man would ever dare to play false, or to reject a lady's advances. In the Sahara, women's rights are strong and they stand by them with wonderful tenacity. The Tuaregs judge a woman by her hair; one with long hair is considered the belle, especially if it reaches to the waist.

The Tuareg women never paint or powder; that is left to the men, who adorn all that part of the face showing above the veil. As a Tuareg man must never uncover his face, the ladies when they want to kiss him do so on his nose, the veil being slightly lowered for the purpose.

No matter how poor they may be, the women do no work, since there are always slaves for manual labour.

In most countries weddings are an occasion for hilarity and expense. This is especially the case with the raiders of the desert when the bride is the belle of the camp. The guests assemble on their huge, cream-coloured camels at the place fixed for the wedding. They arrive from all points of the compass; some may have come from a distance of three or four hundred miles, for it is a great occasion and they are intent on making the most of it. Drums and beautiful hand-made guitars form the orchestra, songs and music are the order of the day, and they also play at the mounted sports which are carried out before the ceremony.

A favourite game at these sports is for one man on an exceptionally fast camel to dash out of the crowd, to be followed by another in full pursuit. The front one will look round, on which his companion behind throws a lance, or it may be a sword, which the other catches in mid-air. It is a great game, yet the Tuaregs never seem to suffer from a cut or severed hand at this extraordinary pastime.

When the festivities are over the guests start on the return journey; their camels can move with amazing swiftness, and although they may have as far to go as from London to Newcastle, they will be there within three days.

They have other curious customs relative to courtship and marriage. The Tuareg girl will sleep for days and nights on end on the tomb of an ancestor, for this will give her a view of her lover who is away on a distant raid, perhaps hundreds of miles down in the all-conquering desert.

These people are a race of natural athletes, and in their flowing robes, each with a sword at his side, a rifle slung over one shoulder, and the eyes peering out from over the closely-fitting veil, they are the typical dwellers in the desert, and look the part.

For food they rely mostly on dates; with a handful of these and a goatskin of water, they will set out, cover vast distances, and return with the proceeds of a raided caravan and a dozen slaves, for which they can get a hundred silver pieces for a man, and as much as four hundred for a young and prepossessing girl. The girl will act as handmaiden to a Tuareg wife, for only one wife is allowed, and although in some things the " People of the Veil " are lax, they study their women to an extent quite unknown among other Eastern, and one might also say, Western people.

Curiously enough, dancing is unknown to them. They look upon it as undignified and not at all in keeping with their proud position as Lords of the Desert.

The question of the origin of the Tuaregs is a fascinating one. Are they of European descent, as has been suggested? At various places in this part of Africa one comes across curious

mementoes of past history. At Niamey, on the Niger, at Rei
Bouba, and elsewhere, one encounters bands of black horsemen,
wearing chain mail and metal helmets. Both men and horses
wear gorgeously coloured quilting as protective armour, and
together with their cross-shaped swords and shields, they make
a picture reminiscent of the days of Saladin and Richard the
Lionheart. Such scenes were probably familiar enough on the
battlefields of Palestine and Syria in Crusading times.

How did this medieval equipment reach the southern Sahara ?
It has been proved that the swords and armour are genuine
enough, for the native African has not got the necessary skill to
reproduce chain mail. They could not have been brought by
ship along the west coast of Africa, for this was absolutely
unknown country five hundred or more years ago. There is
only one explanation. Such weapons and armour must have
been brought overland from the Mediterranean across thousands
of miles of desert. The fascinating question then arises : did
the men who brought them die in battle against the desert
fighters, or did they remain there as the ancestors of the people
we encounter to-day ? Perhaps the Tuaregs are descended from
lost bands of Crusaders who wandered into the Sahara and never
found their way back.

One soon comes to the conclusion that the people who
live here are great wanderers and great fighters—afraid of
nothing but thirst. From Timgad to distant Timbuktu the
tents of the Tuareg beckon, and camel bells tinkle along the
roads leading to those ultimate places where trivial things flee
or fail, and where man is left face to face with awe, immensity,
destiny, and with himself.

It is all illimitable and indescribable ; it is the Sahara and Africa.

CITIES OF SALT

Of all the curious places scattered over the vast surface of the Sahara there is none stranger than that known as the Salines of Argorgott. It is situated five hundred miles from Reggan, the last station on the trans-Saharan motor-coach route. Its other name is the " Inferno of Salt ", and it is ruled over by the Kaid or Lord of Taodeni.

We help ourselves to salt at almost every meal, hardly noticing it, yet becoming immediately aware if it is missing. Although known chiefly as a seasoning for food, salt has many other uses, as we all know, for it is a preservative for fish and meat, is used in the manufacture of soap and sodium compounds, pottery, glass, and many other things, while it is an excellent fertilizer as well as a necessary part of cattle food. In fact, it is one of the essentials in life.

But how many people know of towns made of salt ? Far down in the Sahara there stand two small towns as white as snow—icing towns, like huge Christmas cakes—all made of salt.

Flecker, in the *Golden Journey to Samarkand*, never dreamed of such fantastic places. He wrote :

" Of ships and stars and isles where good men rest,
    Where nevermore the rose of sunset pales,
    And winds and shadows fall toward the West. . . ."

These salt towns are inhabited by people whose origin is unknown. They are said to have come long ago from the north to find refuge from war raids, probably when Islam was being forced on all tribes. Their story is a moving one. They came from the Mediterranean coast where they had lived amid kindly and familiar scenes, but were ousted by the Moors who were by birth and inheritance fighters and pirates, and who forced the Moslem faith on the people wherever they went. So the pre-destined salt-miners decided to pack up and move southwards into the desert to get away from the fanatical armies that were ravishing the country. They were wise, for how any of the inhabitants survived a visitation from the supermen in robbery, arson, and murder, is difficult to explain.

Having nothing else in this barren, isolated spot with which to build their homes, they decided to do it with salt, and so set up their houses of salt blocks. They even constructed the town walls and gateways of salt, as became men of imagination who took what was to hand and made the most of it.

To enter these towns you must pass through a gateway of salt cut into which is a tiny look-out hole. Above, and on the outside, is a camel's skull, the town coat-of-arms. A watcher at the gate scrutinizes all who would enter the salt town, for the people are, from years of isolation, a suspicious tribe, and take no chances.

So secret is its location that you might easily pass within a stone's throw and not be aware of its existence.

Though presenting a picture of cool beauty, these towns are sweltering places in summer, for the salt generates warmth, and there is no relief.

Here they started to mine the salt, which was of outstanding quality. They began to trade with it in certain towns, including Timbuktu. The salt is mined in pure crystals, varying in size from a sugar grain to a small nut, and the tribesmen and their slaves labour at the mining, carting, and packing.

It is used as money, as a medium of exchange for securing the necessities of life. A pinch of salt is the admission fee to the Saharan variety of the Punch and Judy show. You can pay a man's wages in salt, buy food or lodging, or travel long distances with a store of salt to pay your way.

It is a month's journey by camel from Timbuktu to the salt mines of the Salines of Argorgott. The journey takes you across the desert desolation known as El Juf—" The Belly of the Desert ". That sinister name speaks for itself, for many a luckless caravan has been swallowed up in its sun-scorched vastness. That is why the terrible conditions persisted at the salt-mines for so long, for the tremendous distances made it difficult for the French to maintain control over this dangerous and little-explored area. Members of the great caravan from Timbuktu have been massacred several times, despite military protection.

The busy main street of a North
African village, and—

—on the next two pages, a quiet
corner near the bazaar.

Knitting and weaving are occupations pursued as much by men as by women in the Sahara.

A trio in the main street makes music to cheer the passers-by.

Outposts were established in these regions as a preliminary to a regular patrol of the desert, but owing to their inaccessible position the men were condemned to remain alone for unbroken periods of six to twelve months. When relief arrived they were found dead or insane. They had succumbed to *le cafard*, the terrible desert madness. Hundreds more were killed by the desert tribesmen.

Most of the people who work in the salt-mines are virtually the slaves of the Kaid of Taodeni. They come from all parts of the Sahara, and once in the salt city there is no escape. Some are captives taken prisoner during tribal raids, others come from the desert towns. Escape from Taodeni is impossible, for the horizon of the desert is more formidable than a prison wall.

The slaves are neither fed nor paid by their masters, but the proceeds from their labours on every fourth day is allowed them. This they barter for food when the caravan arrives to bring more workers and take back the salt which has been produced. Two pounds of millet costs one bar of salt, while a pound of tea costs twenty-five bars.

Their diet consists almost exclusively of millet and tea. The inevitable result is scurvy in its most virulent form, aggravated by the corrosive action of the salt on the skin and the effect of it in the water they have to drink.

During the day they work in the salt pits, slaving in the heat of the Saharan summer. Their only refuge from the scorching sun and the intense cold at night are the houses and dug-outs built of salt ; here they eat and live and sleep. When at last heat, starvation, and fever have sapped a slave's strength, he stretches himself out on the sand and awaits death with an indifference which seems incredible to the Western mind.

It is certainly well-named " The Inferno of Salt ".

THE FOREIGN LEGION

IN our story of the Sahara we must mention the French Foreign Legion.

The men of the Foreign Legion are the colonizers of the Sahara. I spent many days with them and came to know the corps whose colours are not large enough to contain all the battles and campaigns in which it has fought all over the world.

These men are like the Roman legionaries of old who were soldiers, builders, colonizers, engineers, and pioneers. You can do anything with them, for among them there are architects, engineers, masons, bricklayers, artists, and painters, every one of whom would be needed in constructional work.

A decree of King Louis Phillippe of France in 1831 created the Legion. They were the last of the mercenaries, taking in the veterans of disbanded foreign regiments which had been in the French service.

One of these units was known as the African Auxiliaries, the organizer being a pseudo Belgian baron named Boegard. He collected a number of rogues and rascals, and offered them for service in Algeria where the French troops were having a bad time. This dare-devil crowd were wonderful fighters ; they had nothing to lose but life and quite a lot to gain in the way of loot.

Much sentimental verse has been written on the *Legion Étrangère*, this polyglot force which has an intense *esprit de corps*, with nothing much to look forward to—at the worst, death in the desert, at best, the consciousness of deeds well done and perhaps the *médaille militaire* or some other decoration.

In their hundred and fifteen years they have lost one hundred and fifty-seven thousand men on the battlefield.

Diversity of language is their main feature, coupled with bravery and a wonderful spirit of mutual co-operation. Probably the workmen who tried to build the Tower of Babel were only labour battalions, men much like the Foreign Legion, and that was why, when the confusion of tongues came upon them, their utility ended. Nowadays they would form an admirable draft for the Legion, where difference of language is no bar to enlistment.

The Legion has penetrated the most remote parts of the Sahara. They have opened it up and proved themselves to be the pioneers of the age. There is nothing the Legion cannot do ; from it you could build a ship complete with its engines, staff a university, or run a newspaper ; you could equip a scientific laboratory, man a town-planning body, or a road-building unit, out of this corps of strangers from all over the world. The *legionnaire* is workman as well as soldier. He builds roads and fortified posts, drains marshy areas, and lays out gardens and plantations. He is the mainspring in the expansion of the Saharan empire.

It is far down in the central and southern desert that *le cafard*, as the French call it—boredom—afflicts Europeans. It is a form of desert madness which springs from the sweltering heat, the dust, and the glaring sameness of their environment ; it makes men, especially alcoholic drinkers, do strange things, and even attack each other ; often there is murder in the camp as the result of *le cafard*.

Our sketch of life in the Sahara would not be complete without some mention of the strange characters to be found in the Legion—and what stories they can tell ! I found one to be the cousin of a reigning European monarch ; perhaps he had a difference with his family, or had been told to absent himself over a question of succession. Who knows ? At any rate he had risen to the rank of captain and was making the best of a hard life.

Another was the son of a Russian grand duke ; everything having been lost in Russia when the Bolsheviks took over, there was no room for grand dukes or any of their kin, and so this one wandered on, getting out of Russia by stratagem and disguise, until like human driftage he floated into a common eddy and in the end found himself in the Foreign Legion, with nothing to look forward to in his own country. But it never troubled him ; where he would be when he left the Legion did not matter ; sufficient unto the day was the evil or pleasure thereof.

Another man had served his five years, taken his discharge,

and vanished into some far corner of the earth. He was the son of a European war-time prime minister, but my host felt no surprise at this. The man was a good soldier, he said, and that was all that mattered.

Then there was the mysterious Viennese. A wealthy man had died in Austria and bequeathed his fortune to a nephew . . . but no one could trace the nephew. Then it was suggested that the Foreign Legion should be asked if they had anyone answering to his name and description. When the letter arrived the colonel sent for the sergeant on duty and told him to try to find the missing man. Nothing happened, for, apparently, there was no one of that name and description. Some months later the regiment was in action and the duty sergeant was killed ; sewn up in his tunic were his identity papers which revealed that he was the heir to the fortune. Why hadn't he come forward before ?—a mystery that will for ever be unsolved.

A cousin of the late Kaiser Wilhelm figured in the drama of the Legion. Something had gone wrong and he enlisted under another name. Mortally wounded in battle, he disclosed his identity as death was creeping over him. Telegrams flashed across North Africa and Europe . . . his story was true, and a German warship came to Algiers to take home the body of the common soldier, till then unknown.

I could not find much trace of the advertised brutality of the Legion. I talked freely during my stay in Sidi-bel-Abbes to *legionnaires* of eighteen different nations, of every class and creed, disgruntled men with no very convincing tales of horrors, bored men, and contented men ; and I came perforce to the conclusion that General Rollet's words to me about hit it off. " We are hard, but we are just."

The truth about the Legion to-day would seem to be this. After the inevitable period of hard work for the recruit, the intelligent man who is keen on his job has a not unpleasant time, with promotion and endless opportunities for seeing active service. The man who is stupid, lazy, or mutinous has a distinctly bad time, as, indeed, he would in any army in the world, but not so bad as is commonly made out. Corporal punishment, for instance, is forbidden, and an American lieutenant, who had been through the mill, assured me that men are not tied up, put in holes, and otherwise maltreated. There has been much exaggeration, he said.

The system of training is severe, but it produces fine soldiers, brilliant marchers, and troops always ready for service. These soldiers of fortune can be made use of in the most pestilential climates for the most forlorn hopes, since there is no account to render for their life and death, and no Senate or Parliament to ask embarrassing questions. It may be a vicious system, but its purely military results are unsurpassed.

General Rollet told me that seventy per cent of the Legion are Germans, with Frenchmen, Swiss, Belgians, Bulgarians, Russians, Serbs, Italians, Turks, Czechs, Dutchmen, Cossacks, Britons, and Americans, among others.

I came across about twenty Britons and Americans, as well as a few negroes from the Southern States, but the Anglo-American total in the Legion does not, I was told, exceed a couple of hundred, distributed over the various parts of the French colonial empire where the Legion is in garrison. This is not a great number considering that the strength of the Legion as it is at present totals 23,000 men in eighteen battalions.

Neither the discipline nor the life are suitable to the British and American temperament; I asked the adjutant his opinion of the Anglo-American soldiery in his charge. " They do not take to the life of the Legion like the others," he said. " They are inclined to be independent, and to resent being ordered about peremptorily; but for coolness and reliability under fire—ah! we like to have them in the front line."

One day I found myself in a barrack-room with twenty-eight men, a mixture of eleven nationalities. There was an Englishman, a Scot, three Americans, a Czech, a Siberian Cossack, a Finn, a Bulgar with a beard like a bush, some Germans, a Dutchman, several Frenchmen, a Belgian, a Swiss, and, to wind up with, a Hungarian.

The star turns were the Bulgar and the Siberian Cossack. The gigantic Bulgar spoke in a mixture of Russian and French. He had been far down in the Sahara, where the Legion is constantly at war with the Riffs, the Berbers, and the Tuaregs, marching endless kilometres across the desert in pursuit of these elusive enemies.

He told me of a march through a Saharan sand-storm. All day they toiled along, the seventy-pound packs growing heavier, until the wind made progress impossible. They camped for the night, but when the column stood to arms in the morning one man was missing, a German, who had lagged behind unnoticed.

A sergeant and a dozen men went in search, fear gripping at their hearts, for they knew that none could expect mercy from the Berbers. "They are the children of Hell," said the Bulgar. Two miles away they saw a figure lying in the sand hills. They went forward and shouted, but the figure did not move.

"The sergeant was in front, I came behind," said the Bulgar. "If I hadn't seen the thing with my own eyes I couldn't have believed it. The sergeant stopped suddenly. '*Sapristi!*' he said: 'murdered by the Berbers.'"

They had broken his arms and legs, his face was bashed in, there was scarcely a part of his body that had not been hacked about.

"Yes, they are the children of Hell," said the Bulgar; "but the Legion will not forget."

On the march each *legionnaire* carries a rifle, a bayonet, and 132 rounds of ball cartridge, or rather its equivalent in steel wedges, for live ammunition is not issued except on active service.

Marshal Lyautey was a commander of the Legion, and when the First World War came he took no risks. The regiment that went to the western front contained men of the allied nations only, the Germans being retained in North Africa to keep it quiet.

Later on the Legion had tussles with Abdel Krim, the turbulent Moroccan chief, whose fortitude and military virtue won the respect of his foes. Abdel Krim has another claim to fame. While his guns were rendering to the French attackers his own conception of the *Marseillaise*, he wrote to *The Times*. "The sword is more truthful than writings," he said. "We search for tranquillity and seek only justice ; we remain steadfast to our principles, even if only one mountain-top remain to us to occupy or inhabit."

THE DESERT CORPS

THE French Foreign Legion is often in the news, but there are other desert patrols which lead exciting and romantic lives. The nearest British equivalent is the Desert Corps of the Upper Libyan Desert. It is the duty of this corps to keep the warring tribes under control, and to prevent the smuggling of drugs into Egypt. In its ranks are Britons, Germans, Nubians, and Algerians—all picked men.

Catching drug-smugglers is no light task, for these cunning law-breakers know all the tricks of the trade and never hesitate to fight if necessary. Hashish, a drug made from hemp, was the one the smugglers usually carried. The men of the Desert Corps received six shillings for every pound of hashish captured, and a ninety-pound bonus for each smuggler. But they had to work hard to get this.

The rounding-up of the notorious Hussein Nadir gang was one of their most thrilling exploits. This gang had successfully defied the Desert Corps for several years, and managed to smuggle thousands of pounds of hashish from Libya into Egypt. Though a large number of Secret Service agents were constantly keeping track of their movements, they were always able to slip through the net. When it came to a fight with one of the patrols the smugglers proved too much for the men of the Desert Corps, of whom seven were killed and several others wounded.

Headquarters in Cairo ordered that the Nadir gang be caught at all costs, and the entire six hundred men of the Desert Corps set out into the Sahara. They formed a living chain across the desert, hemming in the bands of smugglers. So swift was the onslaught that the enemy had little time to fight, and Hussein Nadir himself, leader of the gang, was captured.

Another time, a patrol of the Desert Corps followed smugglers for three days into the open, waterless desert. When shooting started the smugglers abandoned the load of drugs, hoping their pursuers would stop to pick it up and thus give them the opportunity to escape. Although torn between the desire to take up the abandoned loads of hashish and to catch the smugglers themselves, the Desert Patrol rode on and, after a fight, succeeded in capturing the gang. Then they rode back to find that a passing Arab had helped himself to the loads of hashish, but he quickly changed his mind when surrounded by the angry members of the Desert Patrol.

These are only a few incidents in the life of this little-known band of men who patrol one of the worst deserts in the world.

Nowadays, as civilization gradually vanquishes savagery, the *legionnaire* and the patrol-man are more emissaries of civilization than warriors. The *legionnaire* builds roads and railways, and his service, advancing with the times, is not the iron tyranny it was said to be. But for years to come he and his comrades will work with both spade and sword, safeguarding the conduits to those reservoirs of African manhood which could give France a powerful colonial army.

§

IRRIGATING THE SAHARA

THERE is another plan for the conquest of the Sahara which, if successful, will be one of the greatest engineering feats ever attempted. Water will be let in from the Bay of Tunis ; at that point a chain of lakes runs necklace fashion for three hundred miles inland. By cutting, digging, and hollowing canals the Mediterranean will be persuaded to supply an inland lake as a reservoir for irrigation. The engineers will be some of those responsible for the inland waterways of Europe and America.

Surely this is a task for Hercules !—harnessing the waters of an ocean to flow over a continent. Imagine for a moment the titanic combat to be staged between water and thirst. The main canal will start from the Gulf of Qabès, a small inlet of the Bay of Tunis. A ridge of fourteen miles in length, and two hundred feet in height, separates the chain of lakes from the sea ; through this it is hoped to cut a canal and form a new inland lake four thousand square miles in extent.

Cedars—on the edge of the Sahara.

Palms make a feathery pattern against the sky.

The canal will be two hundred miles long and forty feet deep, capable of floating ocean liners on its waters. The chain of lakes—Gott el Egeria, Gharsa, and Elneirhir—form the main reservoirs in this engineering feat, while dykes damming up the rivers coming from the south will form subsidiary reservoirs. As the work progresses further wells of water will be created, not to mention the many canals necessary to carry the water into the wilderness, converting it, if plans mature, into agricultural lands of cotton, wheat, and fruit.

It is hoped to harness the Atlantic also, and bring in the waters of that ocean from the west through the defiles of Morocco. Thus two great ideals will co-operate in the conquest of the world's largest desert, transforming it—always provided that the plans of the engineers do not miscarry—into a land of primitive plenty, a land of milk and honey.

The undertaking, greater than any of the old wonders of the world, more dramatic than film stories, will probably have a. marked effect on the hot and dusty climate of North Africa. The winds from the south, which dominate this region, will raise large quantities of water, evaporation being accentuated when the sirocco shrills across the desert. This cloak of moisture moving towards Algeria, Tunisia, and Morocco, may help to tame the desert, tempering its heat during the day, reducing the chill at night, and so making a region of violence more habitable and temperate.

The effects of this undertaking will be almost incalculable. The climate, as we see, may be changed ; the sand will have to come to fruitful terms with the conquering water. The old and puckered face of Africa will lift for an instant with surprise. Certainly the wilderness will begin to blossom like the rose.

But what will the Tuaregs say ?

I talked to some of the veiled desert riders ; I asked them what they thought of the idea of letting the sea fight the Sahara.

They were scornful and suspicious of the moves of modern science. They pointed to the blazing sun. Could I alter that ? They next showed me a camel. Could I change that into a horse ?

I, who have travelled widely, up and down and round the world, and seen some mighty truths shattered by modern invention, could answer nothing. " A man can juggle with little things ; but not with the universe," the Tuaregs declared.

I changed the subject to the topic of veils.

" How did the custom arise ? " I asked.

They stared at me in astonishment. Why did I wear those curious trousers ? I said I hadn't the faintest idea ; and then we all laughed.

The Tuaregs remounted their camels, saying that Allah in his wisdom had not made all men alike, else who would there be left to raid ?

PART TWO   THE KALAHARI DESERT

PANORAMA

"MY Visit to our Stone-Age Forefathers" might well have been the title for this chapter, for in the Kalahari one finds descendants of the prehistoric races that once lived in Europe. Remains of ancestral man have been found in various parts of Europe; here in the South African desert we can find these people actually living to-day. Sometimes in museums you see relics of ancestral man; a canoe, perhaps, made out of a tree-log, or a primitive farming implement. They all seem to belong, however, to a remote past. Yet, among the Bushmen of the Kalahari Desert, you can still see how a tree is felled and made into a dug-out canoe, how hunting, not just for sport but for essential food, is carried on with bows and poisoned arrows, and how the different families spend their lives, not in any kind of huts or buildings, but under shelters made of a few tree branches.

Let us first look at the map of South Africa. There we shall see in the north-western part a shaded area marked "Kalahari Desert". It is this area of the sand-covered inland plateau, called by geographers the Kalahari, of which I shall tell the story. In extent more than half-a-million square miles, it embraces the whole of the Bechuanaland Protectorate, reaches into Angola and touches Northern Rhodesia, and covers areas of South-West Africa and of the northern Cape Province of the Union. Over it the average density of population is less than one person per square mile.

This sandy tract forms an arid plateau, standing over three thousand feet above sea level. The soil is mostly red sand, and there are many sand-dunes. The land is scored by the dry beds of former rivers, but these seldom contain water even in the wet season. Instead, one finds all over the Kalahari large crater-like depressions, called "pans". These collect water during the rains. In fact the name "Kalahari", which is of native origin, means salt-pans.

The headquarters of the administration for the Bechuanaland

Protectorate are at Mafeking, just outside the territory. The total white population of the Protectorate is under two thousand, while the natives number about a quarter-of-a-million. There are no towns as we understand them, merely a few houses at various centres where the European officials and traders live. The largest native village, however, in this part of Africa, is Serowe, the capital of the Bamangwato tribe. Here live about thirty thousand natives.

The main railway line from the south to Rhodesia and the Congo lies along the desert's eastern side; otherwise there is no other railway. There are no roads, only bush tracks, and the dry climate keeps them passable most of the year. Motorists, however, are a rarity. A number of landing-grounds for aeroplanes have been constructed.

Physically the country is far from unattractive. Undulating, with some pleasing scenery in parts, it is mostly covered with bush and grass, and is rich in pasture-grasses of many varieties. It is probably one of the best game countries, both in quantity and variety, to be found in Africa.

Water, or rather the lack of it, is the dominating factor in this land of sand; the rainfall is meagre and irregular in its timing. Such rain as there is falls during the summer months—October to April—but as there is no run-off it soaks away into the sand, and a few hours after a fall has completely disappeared below the surface. The rain, too, is very local; while one area may be drenched, a mile or so away another can be completely untouched.

During the winter the climate is delightful. The sun climbs every morning into a brilliant, cloudless, blue sky; the days are warm and pleasant as English summer at its best; and the nights are cool, even chilly. The winter is the healthiest time of the year in the Kalahari.

Unlike the Sahara, which is about ten times its size, the Kalahari has no mountains and few hills, if one excepts the scattered *kopjes* (small, rocky hills). In the remote past it is believed that this desert was once part of a great forest in which was to be found the Great Ape, and other animals of pre-history. Certainly in the historic past—that is about two hundred years ago—the country was much better watered, for there were lakes then containing water and running streams. But, like many other deserts, the land seems to be drying up more and more each year.

It is difficult, perhaps, for those who have not lived in desert lands to understand how much rain can mean. In the Kalahari the first summer rains are the outstanding event of the year, and men and women, and animals, look forward with an ever-increasing anticipation as the day of their advent draws nearer. Rain means that the dry pans soak in the water, the wells fill up, and the agony of looking for water and finding none is past, for the time being. The wild fruits and succulent water-melon become available to give a change in diet and help build up the ever-scanty food supply.

On the other hand, the rain also brings out more snakes and mosquitoes. In places the tsetse fly becomes more active. But on the whole, the rainfall, meagre as it is, brings new life and vegetation to the desert, and new hopes of survival through the coming dry season.

The heat is excessive in the long summer months, especially in the western portions of the country. The wind blows every day, and always with more or less dust. It is usually calm in the early morning, but rises rapidly, and by the afternoon a small gale may be blowing. By sunset it dies away. Next day is much the same.

Often in the early summer months come whirlwinds, sometimes of large size. The circular motion of the column of wind and dust is rapid but, though unpleasant, is not dangerous. Often you can see three or four of these whirlwinds careering over the country at the same time. Their approach is signalled by a roaring noise, rather like thunder. You turn your back and shut your eyes. If you have time, you tie a cloth round your face to keep the fine sand out of your mouth and nose. Then comes the rush of fine sand, dust, pieces of grass, and bits of stick that are borne along by the wind which feels red-hot. The whirlwind seems to smother you for a few seconds ; then it has gone. It is exceedingly unpleasant while it lasts.

THE PEOPLE IN GENERAL

As regards the people of the country, the first Europeans were Boer hunters in search of game. But they were only visitors. As the Boers settled in the south the game tended more and more to retreat inland away from them and their guns. The Boers followed them. Next came various explorers and travellers. At that time, at the beginning of the nineteenth century, it was thought that the whole of central Africa was like the Sahara. When these early arrivals found themselves in the Kalahari they wrote of its solitude, dust, and lack of water, and this seemed to confirm the idea of its being desert beyond.

Next came missionaries and traders. The best-known of the early missionaries was the Reverend Robert Moffat, father-in-law of Livingstone, who settled at Kuruman on the border of the Kalahari. But the real opening of the country dates from the journey of David Livingstone, Oswell, and Murray to Lake Ngami in 1849. Livingstone exploded the theory about all central Africa being a desert when he discovered the lake and the fertile country beyond. His book, *Missionary Travels and Researches in South Africa* remains a classic of its kind, and is not only very readable but reveals him as an accurate and thorough explorer.

Other travellers, explorers, hunters, missionaries, traders, and mere gold-seeking adventurers followed in Livingstone's footsteps. The country became fairly well known, but it was not till 1885 that a Protectorate was first proclaimed over a portion of what is now known as the Bechuanaland Protectorate, as a result of a pacificatory expedition led by Sir Charles Warren. His main object was to settle the hostilities that had been going on for some time between the natives and the Boers of the South African republics.

Part of the difficulties between the white men and the natives lay in the fact that the Kalahari was a dreamland of wealth. Ideas spread around that in its desert fastnesses were hoards of gold and diamonds. Actually the country has proved barren of this wealth, but at that time all unknown central Africa was believed to be rich in gold. No one would have thought about Bechuanaland and the Kalahari had it not been for the ideas that spread abroad of those supposed hoards of gold and diamonds. All that part of South Africa was rumoured to be auriferous, with the gold mines of Ophir and King Solomon, to which the romantic stories of Rider Haggard lent colour. The mysterious ruins, the stone-built walls, and the mine shafts which had apparently been sunk hundreds of years before the Christian era gave the finishing touches to these legends.

Thereafter the land was miraged with dreams of wealth; but in the end it was all confined to Rhodesia and the Rand, so that Bechuanaland and her people could look upon the operations with philosophical detachment.

Bechuanaland has a history worthy of record, and its career has been dramatic. At the time of Waterloo, the Zulu kingdom was the great menace to South Africa. Chaka, the Zulu chief, so organized his people that they overran large parts of Africa, and either exterminated or controlled the neighbouring tribes. Chaka is said to have been responsible for the death of more than a million people.

It happened that a relation, and one of his leading generals, Moselikatze, fell out with Chaka, having sustained military defeat. Moselikatze left Zululand and set up a separate kingdom, founding the Matabele monarchy. This lasted until 1893, when Lobengula was defeated.

Moselikatze and his supporters pushed as far as the Zambesi and the Kalahari, aiming at the conquest of Bechuanaland. But they did not know their opponents; the Bechuanas and the Bushmen were no match for the Matabele in warfare, yet they could defeat their enemy in another way—by denying him water. On the march the Matabele came to a starvation land, inhospitable and dry. They had pressed into service a number of so-called allies and guides who led the advancing impis on, then faded away, after drawing them on to false trails. The Matabele died in thousands, and the remnants staggered back to their own country. Thirst had done its work, and Bechuanaland was saved.

In the years that followed there was periodic trouble with the

Boers, who were constantly encroaching upon the country, but with the declaration of a British protectorate life in Bechuanaland and the Kalahari went smoothly, until Rhodes and the British South Africa Company—known as the Chartered Company—appeared on the scene. Rhodes had carried a Bill in the Cape Parliament annexing Bechuanaland to the Cape, and he pressed for its transference to the Chartered Company. Just after this move came the Jameson raid, which started from Bechuanaland, and shattered all hopes of that country becoming a Chartered property.

So we come to the time when a picturesque figure had come on to the stage—a great chief of Bechuanaland. His name was Khama, a most astute and go-ahead ruler.

Khama liked the British. So he and some of his tribesmen set out for London to see "the great White Queen"—Queen Victoria—and in accordance with etiquette and red tape they donned top hats and frock coats.

In this garb, which sat as uneasily on them as a coster's feather hat on a Mayfair dowager, they entered the royal presence. They had drafted a curious document, saying what was in their minds. It asked that they might come under British sovereignty, and not be merged in a government under the auspices of Cecil Rhodes. Could not a man be sent among them as the representative of the Queen, one who knew their language and customs, who would be "good-tempered and not impatient", who would love and cherish them? They prayed that the Great White Queen would give this man "the power to become their eyes and ears" and "also our mouth which shall speak our words to you." So it came about that Bechuanaland formed part of the British crown.

Khama had ideas for the conversion of the Kalahari into a land of milk and honey; he saw that water would transform this thirst-land, for where there is water, life and prosperity follow. He propounded these and other progressive ideas on his return.

The journey of Khama and his colleagues to the court of Queen Victoria, and its results, created a stir in South Africa. One of the reactions was that Lobengula, then king of the Matabele, who had laid claim to Bechuanaland, from his fly-ridden kraal in Bulawayo started a correspondence with the

Queen under the huge and impressive elephant seal he had fashioned. But his advances did not bring him addition of territory; moreover, one wonders why he should have cast covetous eyes in the direction of the Kalahari. Perhaps by his letters he was hoping to mitigate the fate that seemed to be in store for him, and at the same time trying to keep faith with the white men, Briton and Boer, who were pressing in on all sides and whose power he surmised.

Khama and his people were deservedly luckier than Lobengula; theirs was a land, not of milk and honey, nor with the glamour of gold, but, with the requisite preparation, it could be one of cattle and sheep, rather than of mine-shafts. This is the compensation which must induce men to penetrate this new land and take on a task of colonization in the desert. Under British rule only a tiny portion, some 7,500 square miles, has been granted for use as European farms; the rest of the territory is either definitely allocated as Native Reserves, or remains Crown Land.

The present native inhabitants of the Kalahari are the Bushmen, commonly called Masarwas, some few Hottentots, and a number of other tribes, all of whom in one way or another are refugees from other parts of South Africa.

Little is known about prehistoric man in the Kalahari. The aborigines of South Africa were the Bushmen, who themselves came from the north, thousands, or possibly even tens of thousands of years ago—it is impossible to say when. These early Bushmen were artists, and their mural drawings are found on rock faces as far north as the Pyrenees and the caverns of the Dordogne in France. Here are the stone men and their descendants—here in the Kalahari.

Succeeding the Cainozoic period, geologists tell us, came four great glacial periods, during which the earth was going through a long universal winter, and it was during this period that the first man-like beings lived upon earth. Forty to fifty thousand years ago, during the final period of the glacial age, creatures with quasi-human attributes appeared and are traceable through bones and flint implements; they were the first dawn men.

Then in European sands were found the remains of a sub-human being at Heidelberg, and others, such as the Neanderthal man in Germany. The Neanderthalers had probably existed for thousands of years ; and then thirty to thirty-five thousand years ago, as the climate of the world grew warmer, a race of kindred beings superior in intelligence to the Neanderthalers came up from the south. None knows their region of origin ; perhaps they were the cavemen of Cro-Magnon and Grimaldi, where the earliest human remains so far known were found.

About twenty-five years ago a skeleton was found on the Rhodesian border, next door to and overlooking the Kalahari, a man intermediate between the Neanderthaler and the real human being. Scientists say that this Rhodesian man is closer to the real man than any other prehistoric skeleton.

Another thing : the skeletons found in the Grimaldi caves were negroid in character ; and their nearest living affinities to-day are undoubtedly the Bushmen of the Kalahari. At the very start of the known story of man, this race from the Grimaldi caves was dark in colour and came from the equatorial south. And these prehistoric people were human to the extent that they pierced shells to make necklaces, drew figures and forms on rocks and in caves, and made life-like sketches of animals. They were hunters, they followed the game as the Bushmen do to-day, they hunted with spears and stones as the Bushmen do to-day, they lived in roughly made shelters. It is presumed that these men hunted over Africa and Europe for perhaps ten thousand years, and then slowly receded south, and kept on going.

The Bushmen were followed by the Hottentots, probably about the thirteenth or fourteenth century, who later on pushed right down to the Cape, and here they were found by the Dutch founder of Cape Town, Van Riebeek, who, with 110 soldiers and artisans, landed in 1652.

The Bushmen, however, acknowledge that there were people in the land before even they came, and they have a strange legend about this race, for they were reputed to be able to swallow ostrich eggs whole. They must evidently have been a giant race—gigantic, at any rate, to the pygmy-like interlopers.

The early settlers regarded the Bushmen and Hottentots as animals, even as vermin—something to be shot at. Little wonder, then, that these primitive creatures should retire as far away as possible from the white man. It was in the desert of the Kalahari that they found sanctuary, but greatly reduced in numbers. As time went on, natives exiled or seeking a refuge from other tribes joined them; but this was hardly an advantage, for the superior Bantus also regarded the original inhabitants as vermin. Every man's hand seemed to be raised in enmity against them.

The Bantu inhabitants, who now form the bulk of the native population, are known as Bechuana, but although members of a single race, speaking the same language, they are far from being a single people. They consist of a number of tribes and sub-tribes, living entirely independent of each other and having their own chiefs. Some of them are regarded as slaves to the stronger tribes, but, in general, each tribe has now its own particular Reserve. The tribal chiefs, acting for the British Government, exercise control, their rule, based on their own ancient customs, being of the fatherly kind and not despotic. Occasionally an unfair or unsuitable chief has to be removed, but the system generally works well.

Christian missions have made certain progress, largely due to the enthusiastic support given by Khama. Many of the natives, and certainly all the Bushmen, have no clearly-defined religion of any kind. They have a vague idea of the existence of an all-powerful spirit; they call this spirit " Modimo ", which has been translated by missionaries as " God ". Witch-doctors, however, abound and exercise great influence. They practise healing, divination, and, of course, rain-making. " Throwing the bones "—rather similar to throwing dice—is reputed to give the witch-doctor signs of what will take place. It is interesting to watch, but it lends itself to all kinds of trickery.

The Bushmen's gods are associated with the things they see around them. There are tree charms, and both good and evil spirits are imagined in daily affairs.

BUSHMEN

THE Kalahari Bushmen are so unique a people that it may be of interest to give further details concerning them and their habits of life.

In size they are small but are certainly not pygmies, the men measuring over five feet in height, the women being slightly smaller. They are fairly muscular and well-developed, but their legs are spindly and they usually have protuberant bellies, owing to the roots and berries on which they mainly live. No one would call them a handsome race, and their faces wrinkle heavily at an early age. A man or woman of thirty will appear to be a hundred years old—a number of them do indeed live a very long time.

The home of the Bushmen is the sort of shelter made of grass and branches by boys in an English garden; only they really live in it. Here the Bushman lives with his wife and family, quite happily, for in disposition they are merry and bright, and they possess a strong sense of humour. Often I have heard them roaring with laughter over some simple thing. They use a drum and a one-string banjo as musical instruments, and are fond of singing; the women often have good voices. Their concerts and dances are, however, lengthy affairs, often carrying on all through the night until the sun is up the following morning.

Clothes do not worry them, and both men and women go about almost naked. They are fond, however, of bangles and necklaces, and you can give a Bushman no finer present than two or three meat-tin openers, which he will either stick in his ears or string on to a necklace. They do not want boots, for their feet are as hard as leather and much more pliable. They never wash, but occasionally clean their teeth with a stick, and the women now and then have a " wash " by sprinkling dust over themselves ! This they generally do prior to a dinner or a dance.

In dancing the ladies usually make up the orchestra ; they are critical of the dancing technique of the men and freely express their approval, or otherwise. Singing goes on to the tune of the band, which comprises reed flutes and an instrument that looks like a bow, with the shell of a tortoise, which is the Bushman equivalent of a sound-box ; and, primitive though these instruments are, they get good musical effects from them. The Bushmen seem to have a natural flair for music, and pick up tunes whistled to them, reproducing them in their own playing.

When courting, the Bushman has original ideas on the way to win the bride. They are in keeping with desert laws and the ever-present food-problem. When he has his eye on the belle of the camp, or that of a neighbouring family, he must ingratiate the father of the girl. This he does by stalking and killing a large animal, such as an eland antelope, a good specimen of which may weigh up to six hundred pounds. Having done this he comes to the father and places his spear, or bow and arrow, on the ground, fresh from the kill, to indicate the success he has had. In other words he has " to deliver the goods " ; and then the girl is his.

Sometimes the father is exacting and requires the lad to pursue a particular animal and bring it to book within sight of the encampment—no easy job. The candidate goes forth, stalks a giraffe or some other mighty game as directed, wounds it with his arrow and then turns it in the direction of the lean-to home. It requires consummate skill to do this, but in the end the Bushman triumphs and the game is brought within fairly close range of the goal. The family goes out, showers congratulations, and the equivalent of the marriage bell rings out merrily.

Each family, and the new families created by marriage, has its own allocated territory, based on the food and water supply. There is method here ; for if feuds break out between families, the fight never takes place on the home pitch but on some arid adjacent ground where the innocent shall not suffer. This community organization is dictated by the desert, and each family or group concentrates solely on its own small circle of life and death.

It follows that there is no system of government with the Bushmen ; the only form of authority is parental, and even that the young Bushman discards when he is grown up. He goes out into the wilderness to follow his own devices, much the same as an animal does, when parental protection is no longer required. The children are brought up in an animal way, and from the first day must be able to shift for themselves. With no parental guide to help them they scatter over the face of the land and fend for themselves, in keeping with the law of necessity.

When grown-up, the men usually have a small game horn hung round their necks, containing medicine or snuff. Many also have filthy clay pipes. Everything about them is filthy, and they are literally caked with dirt and grime. They smear themselves with rancid fat, which does not add to their attractiveness, for it makes them smell horribly. They mix red and white clay with the fat and then rub it all over their heads, faces, and bodies. Bushmen certainly do not mind each other's smell or appearance, and claim, in fact, that this fat helps to keep them cool in summer and warm in winter.

Their language is primitive, consisting of various kinds of clicks, and only an expert linguist can understand them. Their vocabulary is limited, and they can count only up to three. To hear two Bushmen shouting out to each other across the *veld* is rather like listening to baboons having a row. An ancient writer has described their language as " something like the screeching of bats ".

As the Kalahari Bushmen are living practically in the Stone Age, they have little tribal organization. Each family goes its own way. The father rules the roost until such time as he loses his physical powers, and then he is displaced. Civilization with its restrictions is unendurable to them. They must have freedom, and it has been found impossible to get them to adapt themselves to carrying out any laws. Even when they have to go to prison for some serious crime they pine away, unless the jail warder lets them out daily to go hunting for their own roots and wild berries. Contrary to its practice with all other natives, the Government has also found it impossible to tax them. A few Bushmen have been tamed enough to be employed in herding cattle, but they are apt to disappear suddenly when they hear the call of the wild.

Father lends a hand: a male ostrich takes on
the job of hatching the eggs.

A herd of eland raise the dust of the Kalahari as a
plane flies low over them.

Wildebeest and zebra too scatter across the desert
from such an unfamiliar sound.

Their household possessions are few—two or three pots to cook their food in, a few spears, bows and arrows, some skins, ostrich-egg shells to hold water, and perhaps a knife or two. They make clay pots, but prefer now to trade game skins for an iron one at the nearest store.

Fire is made with fire-sticks of different kinds of wood, the larger of soft wood and the smaller of a harder type. The method of producing the fire is this : the Bushman places the soft piece of wood on the ground and holds it firmly with his feet ; a small notch made in it takes the sharpened end of the piece of hard wood, which is as thick as an ordinary pencil ; the drill-wood is then twirled rapidly between the hands until smoke is seen and the wood begins to glow, when it is covered with a piece of moss, on which the Bushman blows. The moss catches fire, and cooking can begin. It takes a Bushman only a few minutes to make such a fire ; others can with considerable effort create smoke, but to get a glow is an art.

The Bushman has a gift for detecting water almost as if he himself were a long-range divining rod. I remember once we went for twenty-eight thirsty hours without a sign of anything liquid, until our water-finders found a few shallow water-holes among the bush and scrub. No glass of champagne ever went down better. We had almost arrived at the final gasping stage, while our horses were even worse. On reaching the water they whinnied, begged, and cajoled until their turn came, when a stampede of school children would have been mild compared with their rush for refreshment.

So precious is water here that Bushmen put it in ostrich eggs, filled through a small hole, and hide it in the sand. They leave no signs, but know the spot by instinct. They have many ways of finding water and in likely places will drive down a long hollow reed, and suck up the liquid. These holes are known as " sip water ", and the remarkable thing is that if one digs for water on the exact spot it is not to be found.

These strange beings do not know what a bed is, and when they want to go to sleep they just scoop out the earth and coil themselves up in a small hole, with their knees drawn up to their chins. They can also sleep soundly while squatting on their heels near a fire. Sometimes they topple over and get burnt, but this never seems to worry them. In lion country they may even sleep in bivouac under the trees, with the heavens for a canopy, and the stars for lamps ; the wood fire cooks their meal, and they know just where to find water ; and mosquitoes and sand flies seem to drop off after one bite, for the effluvium of these people is too strong, even for a mosquito.

The change of domicile is constant, and so, living like wild animals of the jungle, the lean-to arrangement is the solution to the housing problem. The materials are there to hand, and in a few minutes the house is ready for occupation. When, within a week or ten days, the neighbouring ground is devoid of game, they move on and repeat the process elsewhere. Since the dawn of history they have been doing the same thing, and time has not altered the picture or the plans.

When within earshot of a Bushman camp, a warning shout must be given, otherwise poisoned arrows will come spinning through the air. The Bushmen are suspicious creatures and they want to know who the visitor is before admitting him.

In their migrations in search of water, Bushmen tend to follow the antelope. Sometimes, when hungry, they look at the sky for vultures. Vultures mean the lion's kill, where may be found the marrow bones of giraffe and other game of considerable size and succulence.

What of religion ? These simple people, clothed in about as much as you could put into a matchbox, have no wicked practices, such as the head-hunting of the Sumatrans or the " smelling-out " and murderous rites of the Central African witch-doctors. They pray to no god, but offer simple oblations, and the spirits, they believe, rule the elements and the sources of sustenance.

The Bushmen never cultivate anything, least of all themselves. They neither sow nor reap. Nature has, however, provided them with her own food, mainly roots, berries, and melons. The melons are prolific, and both men and animals thrive on them. There are two species, similar in appearance, but while one kind is tasteless, the other is bitter. Animals will eat both, but the Bushmen enjoy only the tasteless kind, eating them both raw and cooked. Often they bury a store of melons to see them through the dry season.

Hunting, however, is not only their main occupation in life ;

it also provides them with their favourite food. They hunt game with clubs, spears, and bows and arrows. The arrows are tipped with poison which is made in various ways. It is obtained from the poison of snakes, a special kind of slug, or from the juice of a local tree. In each case the poison is mixed with a binding agent, and the final mixture kept in small moulds until such time as it is required. The manufacture of the poison is accompanied by the chanting of weird songs, for this is supposed to increase the power.

Hunting, practised almost from the time a youngster begins to walk, has developed the Bushman's power of observation. He will track down an animal by its claw marks on a tree, or by watching the flight of mosquitoes. He will catch a bee, gum a tiny feather or a piece of down on it, and follow its flight through the bush, from shrub to shrub and flower to flower, until the honey store is found.

With the larger animals the Bushmen have a special technique. To catch them they burn the grass, where there is any, so that it will spring up afresh and attract the game to the locality. In anticipation of this they will have previously dug concealed pits from which to open fire at the right moment with their bows and arrows.

They stalk animals in an animal way, almost like a cat, and when it is a case of following up game they run on tirelessly for hours on end, and literally succeed in running down their quarry by the simple process of tiring it out. After a spectacular kill they celebrate with a feast, and dancing, for men only, dramatizing the antics and habits of various animals, their eating, drinking, and fighting ways, and how they dash for safety in moments of danger. Some of these plays reach a high level of skill in mimicry.

The Bushmen are just as much a part of the jungle and the desert as the wild animals themselves. At tracking they are unsurpassed; to them the bush and scrub are an open book, and they know every sign and portent. Step by step they move forward on successive stages of the trail. Their bare feet touch the ground so lightly that they seem to float through space, past-masters of the tracking art, a living part of the bush and the desert.

G 2

Nothing whatever escapes their eyes, trained by years of scouting and backed by an age-old instinct. Slowly and noiselessly they creep on ; here a branch has been swept aside and is in an unnatural position ; a tiny spot of blood may be on a leaf, and to them it is a wondrous tale ; a blade of grass has been disturbed, or a tiny hair may be spotted on a thorn bush. With senses keyed up to the highest pitch they keep all the time an intensive look-out for any sight or sound that will give the first intimation of the animal's whereabouts.

Should the ground be bare and open near his quarry, the Bushman will crawl along, taking advantage of every hollow in the ground, and sometimes holding a small branch of bush in front of him. Slowly he goes closer and closer. The game, seeing only a piece of bush, takes no heed, especially as the hunter is careful to be on the leeward side. When he has got as close as he thinks possible without really alarming the animal the Bushman gets his bow and arrow ready. He shoots his arrow—and then lies flat again. He does not want to stampede any of the other animals that may be in the herd.

The poisoned arrow may take effect very quickly, but it depends on the poison that has been used. Some of the poisons kill only after some hours. Perhaps the animal is only slightly wounded and attempts to escape ; it may be possible to get in another arrow-shot. Sometimes the hunter must follow his wounded prey many miles before coming on its dead body. He keeps it up for hours, never allowing the animal to rest until it drops.

My friend, the late F. C. Selous, one of Africa's most famous big game hunters, who knew the Kalahari well, came across a Bushman who, after a long stalk in the heat of the day, had with his bow and arrow wounded a bull eland. Selous estimated that the Bushman followed the eland for fifty miles ; he was tireless in the pursuit, until finally his quarry collapsed. Our hunter then covered it up with grass and bush, and went back as far as from London to Brighton to tell his family and call them up to the feast.

By the time the family had reached the eland the hunter must have covered a hundred and fifty miles, and we can imagine the state of the eland by that time! It would certainly be in an advanced stage of putrefaction. Twenty-four hours at least must have elapsed since its death, and all that time the carcase was lying in the sweltering heat covered with millions of flies. The fact that the meat may be high and fly-blown matters not at all, however, to the Bushmen. On this particular occasion they dined well, staying on for a further day or two until every bit of meat was eaten. They cracked the marrow-bones for the marrow; the skin they took back to their home and hung in a tree, for hungry days might come and then, like Magellan and his sailors who, in the first circumnavigation of the globe, chewed the boiled sails, the Bushmen might have to exist by chewing eland skin until the coming of a good hunting day.

For killing birds and small game the Bushman uses the native knobkerrie. With grea skill he will knock over a bird either sitting, running, or flying, and up to a distance of fifty yards. Pits are also dug in which to trap big game. They are placed along the paths used by the animals to reach their drinking pools. These are funnel-shaped, narrowing at the bottom which is some six feet deep. Often a poisoned stake is placed in the pit. Then it is covered with loose branches and grass. In order to make sure of a victim several such pits may be dug, so that if an animal suspects one he then unsuspectingly tumbles into another. There is seldom any chance of escape. As may be imagined, the work of constructing these pits is considerable, for the Bushmen possess only the most primitive tools. Time, however, is of no importance to them.

The only animals the Bushmen possess are dogs, and these are also used in hunting. They are savage, hungry-looking mongrels. They follow their masters on the chase, and will tackle with astounding courage leopards and hyenas. They are carefully trained how to behave during hunting expeditions.

We are apt to look on the Bushman menu with horror. Yet his tastes are not more unusual than the frogs and snails of France, the shark's fins at a Chinese banquet, or the caviare which the native of northern Siberia disdains. It is said that there is nothing new under the sun, but apart from a Bushman feast I have attended dinners that had a certain novelty and go to prove how relative are such matters as eating and drinking. Lizards roasted on the point of a spear are a delicacy in the Australian desert ; grubs that are skinned like a prawn ; and rats with the fur picked off and the meat roasted on the red-hot ashes, with an *entrée* of snake meat, is a meal that is a novelty but not a gastronomic delight.

Bushmen will crack and swallow the contents of eggs that are just ready to hatch, or that are already rotten. I sometimes felt quite ill at the smell of these eggs, but the Bushmen say : " It is not the stink but the egg that we eat." Their other luxuries include lizards, snakes, locusts, and wild honey. They are practically omniverous, hunger compelling them to use everything catable, both animal and vegetable. Their appetites are formidable, and I have wondered at their digestive powers. Three or four Bushmen will polish off a three-hundred-pound buck antelope at a sitting, and could still eat more ! They half roast the kill, removing the small area around the poisoned part if an arrow has been used. Nothing is wasted or left, except the bones.

You could learn more about hunting in a day with a Bushman than in a month or more browsing among books. You would hear that the lion is a great walker, pacing majestically through the bush, head down, feet treading velvet footsteps ; and you would get another picture of the lion roaming the bush, muscles relaxed, senses alert, with a roar that awakens the world. The roar is, in a sense, a form of thanksgiving for food, or it serves to call up the lion's wives and friends to the banquet. Sometimes it is a sign that his suspicions have been aroused. No four-footed beast has such eyesight as the lion. His pupils at night swell into glowing lamps. Like the tiger he has one failing : his sense of smell is nearly non-existent.

There is another, smaller inhabitant of the Kalahari scrub jungle, the porcupine, having many virtues and, as far as I found, no vices. It is not easy to catch, for it can use its sharp-pointed quills. The Bushmen, however, know that a blow on the sensitive nose kills it. When roasted the porcupine makes excellent eating, not unlike pork, and is esteemed a delicacy.

This concludes what I have to say of the Bushmen. There are not many of them left in the world to-day—perhaps only two or three thousand. But there are signs that they are no longer decreasing in numbers, thanks to the interest and care now taken of them by the Administration. They have many faults, but are human and loyal to anyone they really trust. They are one of the keys to the Stone Age, and knowing them and their habits and customs helps us to understand our own savage ancestors. It is doubtful if they can long remain a separate race. Already quite a number are being absorbed by the surrounding tribes, and there are many half-breeds. If they do disappear, one of the most interesting races will have vanished from the earth.

§

HOTTENTOTS AND DAMARAS

THERE are not many pure-bred Hottentots to be found now in the Kalahari Desert. Like the Bushmen, being non-Bantu, they fled from Cape Colony owing to the treatment received at the hands of early settlers. A few elements, however, are still to be found there.

While the Bushmen are hunters, the Hottentots are one stage higher in the scale of civilization, being nomads and owning flocks of cattle and sheep. In turn they are one step lower than the Bantu, who are agriculturists.

In appearance the Hottentots resemble the Bushmen, but are slightly taller. They possess a similar cunning in hunting game. Like them, they anoint their bodies with rancid fat mixed with clay. Their feeding habits are not quite so dirty, and the milk from their cows is their principal food, together with meat, berries, roots, and honey. They do not use bows and arrows, but prefer guns, and their clothing consists of skins, skin caps, and, in the cold weather, sandals.

The Hottentots' housing is an improvement on that of the Bushmen, for they have huts made of sticks stuck in the ground, and covered with grass or reed mats; otherwise there is little extra comfort. Their great interest in life is cattle; it is their form of wealth. These cattle are much inferior to those of Europe, but are hardy and suited to desert conditions. The oxen are trained to be ridden and to carry household goods when a tribe is on the move. The youngsters when in want of a drink of milk help themselves, catching a goat or sheep and squirting the milk from the teat into their mouths. The boys also have races, each riding his own particular ox.

The Hottentots possess a fund of superstitions and folklore. Moon-worship among them has been an organized religion, and some have a belief in immortality. They have a great fear of ghosts, and consider that any place which has been the scene of death by violence at once becomes a ghost's permanent residence, and that such a spot must be carefully avoided.

Another indication of their superiority to the Bushmen is that they understand the meaning of laws, pay native taxes, and also work for Europeans. They are good with cattle, faithful to those employers who treat them well, and take pride in their charges. It is hard, indeed, to find better herdsmen in South Africa.

Their language is outwardly similar to that of the Bushman, for it consists of clicks. Actually it is more elaborate and complex and has a wider range of expression. They can count much further.

Despite these higher accomplishments they are, however, a dying race.

Another interesting desert people—although, like the Hottentots, few in number—are the Damaras or Hereros. They are comparatively recent arrivals, for their original home was over the border in South-West Africa. At the beginning of this century, when the latter territory belonged to the Germans, fighting broke out. The Germans almost exterminated the tribe, reducing them from fifty-five thousand to about sixteen thousand. They committed frightful barbarities on these unfortunate natives, and drove them out into the desert to perish of thirst. Some managed to escape into British territory where they took service under the Batawanas, another Kalahari tribe. They made themselves useful, especially with cattle. In time the Damaras acquired large herds of their own, possibly by dubious methods, and having become rich they repudiated servitude with their masters.

The Damaras are a tall people, many of the men being over six

A Bushman fills his water-bottle—an ostrich egg.

Windhoek, South-west Africa, a town on the edge of the Kalahari.

A typical stretch of scrub country in the Kalahari Desert.

Bushmen still make fire by one of the oldest
known methods.

feet in height. They have extraordinary customs, the most striking being the wearing of a peculiar head-dress by the women. Made of leather, it is heavily ornamented with iron beads ; in front is a curtain of leather, a head-piece with lappets, and artificial strands of fibre are plaited into the hair and left to hang down in long plaits. The origin of this weird head-dress is unknown, but it is similar to a Viking helmet. The Damaras attach great value to them and are unwilling to sell to a white man even when offered a high price.

The men also go in for long plaits of artificial tresses, plastered with fat and clay. This form of hair-dressing is certainly hot and uncomfortable, but such is the force of custom that they would not dream of giving it up.

The Damaras are an objectionable people, being insolent, quarrelsome, and filthy ; but they are intelligent, and capable with cattle. The women have a curious method of collecting their principal food, which is the eggs of white ants ; they weave shallow baskets, through which the sand is sifted, the eggs remaining behind.

By far the greater part of the native population consists of the Bechuanas, and even this name covers at least thirty different tribes of varying strength. The term Bechuanas means men who have escaped, for originally they came to the Kalahari in order to get away from their original homes. Some of the tribes are of poor type, being little superior to the Bushmen. The largest and the most superior are the Bamangwatos, who are skilled agriculturists and stockfarmers. The general poverty of the Bechuanaland Protectorate, however, compels many of the more enterprising of the young men to leave their desert homes and seek profitable employment in Johannesburg and elsewhere in the Union.

TRAVEL IN A THIRSTY LAND

When Livingstone made his first famous journey across the Kalahari to reach Lake Ngami his greatest problem was the lack of water. For transport he used wagons drawn by oxen, but these were abandoned owing to the water problem, and he had to continue on foot. Out of fifty oxen he lost forty-seven.

Every traveller since then—excepting, of course, those who merely fly over the desert by aeroplane—has had to face the same difficulties. The motor-car over certain main routes has been of great assistance, but even cars get stuck in the sand or fall into hidden ant-holes, possibly breaking an axle. Then the traveller finds himself stranded a hundred miles or more from the nearest water. There have been many tragedies of this kind.

One of the saddest and greatest of such tragedies took place about fifty years ago. Far out on the western Kalahari is one of the loneliest white settlements in Africa. This is Ghansis, founded by Cecil Rhodes, and forgotten after his death, but still struggling against isolation. There are less than two hundred white settlers at Ghansis, which even to-day is difficult to reach, for it is cut off by the desert.

When Rhodes heard of good ranching country in this distant corner of the Kalahari he decided to establish a white colony there. His motives were partly political, for at that time the era of German colonial expansion was in full swing, and Rhodes wished to forestall them. German expansion might have threatened his dream of a Cape to Cairo railway, whereas a buffer British territory would protect it. So Rhodes offered to give volunteers free ten-thousand-acre farms, a full supply of equipment, food stores, and a gift of £200 for each family.

Sixty families accepted this offer, and three hundred men, women, and children set out to reach the land of promise. Few survived the dreadful trek which was marked by successive disasters. Mile after mile their route was marked by heaps of stones under which they buried their dead. Disease killed off most of their cattle. Heavy sand slowed down their progress

so that often the wagons covered only half-a-mile a day. Bushmen attacked the column, killing several people in it with their
poisoned arrows, while lions seized some of the men who went
off into the bush in search of game. Others got lost in the same
search. In the swamp areas malaria claimed its victims.

But the danger and problem that never left them was the
shortage of water. This was the thought that filled their minds
day by day. Often when they did arrive at an expected well it
was only to find that it was dry or muddy. Each stretch of this
nightmare journey took its toll ; only the strongest succeeded in
reaching their destination. The covered wagons arrived at
Ghansis on Christmas Eve, 1898.

For nearly sixty years the brave and hardy settlers have had to
face loneliness and every kind of hardship. The nearest doctor
is two hundred miles away. Mails sometimes take several weeks
to reach them, and supplies such as flour, coffee, and sugar get
lost on the way. The motor-car now has improved their
position ; but getting their cattle to the Johannesburg market is
still difficult, and in a dry season the trek across the great thirst-
land of the Kalahari Desert takes its toll of hundreds of animals.

Ghansis is shown on the map. It is about one hundred miles
south by west of Lake Ngami, and when you arrive there it is
to find a settlement, with only a magistrate's office, a post office,
police post, and a store. Wireless keeps this small community
in touch with the outside world, for there is, as yet, no telegraph
or telephone.

On the scattered farms cattle have to be protected from lions
at night by means of strong stockades. Every boy and girl
almost lives in the saddle and knows how to handle a rifle. The
only regular social event is the fortnightly arrival of the mail,
when people travel into Ghansis to meet each other and exchange
farming and other news. A dance is a rare event, and cinemas
and similar amenities are unknown.

It would take several days to reach Ghansis from Ngami by a
properly tractored motor-car ; it is a lonely journey over a sandy
track that winds through burnt-up grass and scrub bush, with the
ever-prevalent dust and whirlwinds. Toiling along you see
wild game of every description watching the passing traveller,
seemingly without fear. Now and then frightened Bushmen

peer from behind rocks and bushes. They will come out, however, when offered a gift of tobacco. At last you reach Ghansis, which seems to be a paradise after the country passed through. Here there are windmills and water, homes and gardens, cattle and human beings.

For those who have not experienced it or felt the call, it is hard to understand the force that draws certain men and women to spend their lives in the desert and wilderness. Is it to escape from a world which is too material, too selfish?

Even in the Kalahari, as elsewhere in isolated places, there are hermits. One such lives beside a desert pan. His home consists of a couple of native huts which he has furnished comfortably. On the walls are magnificent karosses. This seventy-year-old German has lived there for twenty-five years, trekking, hunting, doing some trading. Wars do not interest him, for he has disappeared into spaces which even war fails to reach. What he has heard about modern warfare only seems to have confirmed his dislike for civilization. He has no desire ever to leave his desert home, over two hundred miles distant from his next white neighbour.

Another used to disappear into the Kalahari Desert for months at a time. No one knew where he went or what he did there. He lived in the territory so long that there can be few corners he has not explored. But he did this for his own pleasure. His permanent address might almost have been " Out in the Blue ".

Crossing a hundred-mile waterless stretch of the Kalahari with an ox-wagon is no mean feat. This is how a police officer described the means by which he used to achieve it. He took his wagon ten miles along the route, outspanned his oxen and had them herded back to the starting-point, where they drank. They were then grazed forward to where the wagon stood. The next day the oxen drew the wagon another ten miles, and again they returned alone to the starting-point for drinking. They then had to graze forward twenty miles to reach the wagon. This method would even be repeated for a third stretch, although this time perhaps only five or six miles might be covered.

There now followed a continuous trek of fifty miles without any water for the oxen. Most of the travelling was done during the cool evening, the night, and early morning. The journey started at half-past-four in the afternoon. At half-past-seven there was a halt, when the oxen were outspanned, grazed, and rested. At nine the journey was resumed until midnight, when there was a further halt until three o'clock. At six, when it was dawn, a few more miles would be covered, and at nine the oxen were rested until the afternoon came round again.

By almost superhuman efforts the oxen had now covered fifty miles without water, apart from a little moisture from the dew at early dawn. These oxen were locally bred and had been trained to go long distances without drink. But after this fifty-mile stretch they could draw the wagon no further, being "dried out". They were able, however, to travel unharnessed to their destination, get watered, and trek back, grazing, to the wagon. Refreshed, they drew it for ten miles, and the performance by which they had covered the initial stages of the journey was repeated. Such a trip is slow, but it achieves the object of getting stores through to a lonely post.

When an ox drops exhausted on the way, things happen. There is almost sudden action—a dramatic descent from the skies above. Within a matter of minutes vultures appear seemingly from nowhere. Even the learned in the science of ornithology cannot explain this vulturine bolt from the blue—tiny specks at an enormous height, circling round, and literally dropping from the skies, when there was never a sign of life before. Either the eyesight of the vulture must be something beyond the grasp of the human mind, or they are gifted with a sixth sense of which we, as yet, know nothing.

The first thing a vulture does when it alights on the carcase is to pick out the eyes, as if conscious of the fact that once deprived of sight the animal is at its mercy. Many a man lost in the desert, and who has collapsed from physical exhaustion, has had a hard and grim fight with vultures before convincing them that he is no mere carcase. Conversely, this coming of the vultures and their gathering in the skies is a signal to the watchers in the desert that something is amiss, and lives have been saved by following this sign.

The Kalahari is a land of surprises, and in nothing more so than in its Camel Corps, the riders of the desert, who keep watch and and are responsible for many things. They are the outward and visible sign of authority, the mounted police, who maintain law and order in the desert. Yet they number only thirty European officers and N.C.O.s with about three hundred native police. This tiny body represents the might of the British Empire in a country more than twice the size of Britain.

Often the members of the force are away from their base for a couple of months at a time, and during this period they never see another European or come in contact with the amenities of civilization. They are cut off from the world ; newspapers and the radio are no longer of interest to them ; only the desert and its mysteries occupy their time and attention. The patrols consist of a couple of Europeans and half a dozen trained natives, and when setting out they can never be certain of returning. They are in the hands of destiny. Their time is spent in wandering ; adventure beckons, and they follow.

How small man and all his works must seem when the patrol plunges into the unknown ! What does the future hold for them ? Man is a small thing, here to-day and gone to-morrow ; but the desert is always there. At night they camp by a water-hole ; the moon shines calmly and clearly and the air is comparatively cool, but on the morrow the sun will come up again in all its fiery heat as they strike camp, and like a ship sail on again. For them the unknown has its light and darkness and its promise of adventure ; and to these men who roam the desert there is a depth of magical and wonderful allure. What do they do when they are out on patrol ?

To begin with they are facing the unknown. In ages long past men ventured into the unknown and brought back knowledge and wisdom ; they fought and overcame wild men and animals ; they often had a long struggle with Nature and the calamities she can provide. Of such men are the camel corps composed ; they collect taxes from native villages and watch out for rinderpest, the scourge of South African cattle, which has swept away untold numbers of stock. Then there is the locust ; always the patrol keeps a look out on the skyline for the coming of this pest, and is often able to send a timely warning.

The locusts in this part of Africa are Public Enemy Number One ; they appear after the rains have brought out the green grass and growing crops, and descend in dense clouds, sometimes miles in length. They eat everything green that comes their way—corn, grass, vegetables, fruit. Not a vestige remains. It is almost impossible to believe until one has seen this great enemy of South Africa. Even a railway train gets held up if a locust swarm crosses its path. They crawl over the rails and, having oil in their bodies, prevent the train wheels from gripping.

There is, however, one bright side to a locust invasion. Both natives and stock revel in eating the devastating pest. We know from the Bible how people lived in the desert on locusts and honey. This is no exaggeration : to the natives the locust is a tasty luxury. Stock of all kinds rush round when locusts are on the ground, gobbling them up alive. This helps milk-production, and the hens lay many extra eggs.

The desert police accustom themselves to controlling thirst. They know that possibly one day a period of thirst will face them, demanding every ounce of strength and stamina to pull them through. Even the camels, which do particularly well in this part of Africa, go through a training in abstinence, for if they do become accustomed to regular drinking they do not last long when out in the desert. As it is they can carry on for four or five days without water.

Travel kit is cut down to a minimum, and consists of tea, condensed milk, a small stove, blankets, and a rifle—meat is obtained by shooting game. This kit is carried on spare camels, along with specially-made iron tanks carrying a supply of drinking water. Some patrols they make are quite waterless, and may be two hundred miles in length. They cover usually about forty miles a day, travelling at five miles an hour, visiting solitary groups of Bushmen who see a white man only once a year. The men of the Camel Corps are not rich, but they seem content with the simple life the desert offers as its attraction.

Apart from thirst, there are other perils to be faced when travelling in this desert. Unless you have a competent guide, nothing is easier than to be lost. Some time ago an aeroplane of the Royal Air Force lost its bearings and crashed in the desert. The airmen escaped injury only to be killed by poisoned arrows shot at them by hidden Bushmen. Their bones were discovered some time later, but their murderers were never traced.

Desert madness, which the French in the Sahara call *le cafard*, may attack a man in the desert even if he has company. The awful loneliness seizes him and he becomes mad.

After the lack of water, snakes and scorpions are the worst desert enemies. A man may even find on waking that a snake has curled up beside him under his blanket for warmth. It takes great presence of mind to act correctly without a moment's delay, and safety allows no hesitation, for many of these snake have a deadly bite. Scorpions also thrive under desert conditions, and it is easy to tread on one unawares.

There is a treatment for snake-bite which is successful if carried out in time, although the shock itself might be enough to kill some people. The Bushmen have their own special antidote, consisting of powdered lizard. They make two cuts, one above and one below a bite, and rub a little of the powder into them ; they also put a little into some water and drink it. Personally, I believe this treatment is efficacious, for I have never heard of a Bushman or Hottentot dying from a snake-bite.

The Kalahari can stage an unusual display of electric atmospherical disturbances, startling to the European traveller.

After heavy rain, the sky is as highly charged with electricity as the earth with green in time of spring, and the desert is turned into an electric power-house. When the yellow, mauve, and orange lightning has ceased, the ground takes on the pattern of display. Miniature sparks fly from animals as they leap through the scrub jungle, and the headlights of their eyes at night are no brighter than the sparks that fizzle from their skins, for all the world like a cracker in a child's hand. A moving ox-wagon can assume a luminous appearance. The native driver might be wearing a kaross—the skin of a leopard—and if he rubs it, sparks fly off. I have heard of people in the Canadian winter rubbing their carpet slippers on the floor and then lighting the gas ring. One finds this hard to believe, but after seeing the Kalahari, there is no room for doubt. Here you can see the primitive Bushmen and Hottentots in skins lit up like glow-worms, and vegetation and sky bewitched with theatrical lighting effects.

Motor-cars are now the main means of communication between various centres and posts. They are fitted with balloon tyres to enable them to get through the sandy tracks, and it requires skilled drivers to ensure no sticking. It is a tough job on a broiling hot day to extricate a car which is embedded in sand.

You must, of course, if going out on any expedition or long journey, take not only water, but full supplies of spares in case of eventualities. You may be sure that something untoward will occur, for there is little smooth going. A car that can stand up to a prolonged Kalahari trip is worthy of the highest testimonial.

For minor transport and journeys to solitary places donkeys are often used, being tough and able to carry a fair load. Sometimes the native postman travels on foot, with pack-donkeys carrying the mail.

In places you may have to wait weeks for a reply to a letter. The best example I have ever heard of concerned a young man on the eastern side of the Kalahari Desert whose fiancée lived about 450 miles away—a little more than the distance between London and Glasgow. Each letter the young man wrote went south first by train, then northwards to Windhoek, the capital of South-west Africa. From there it went east to the railhead at Gobabis, whence the native postman set out on his two hundred-mile journey to reach the settlement where the girl was living. A letter from one lover to the other took a month on its journey, if all went well. Yet it cost only three-halfpence.

The Bechuanaland Protectorate has its own picturesque stamps, and its issues are eagerly sought after by stamp collectors all over the world.

§

THE ANIMAL KINGDOM

THROUGHOUT the Kalahari there are numerous wild animals, dependent, like man, upon the rainfall, but far better equipped by Nature to withstand the lack of it. This wild life, as I have shown, contributes to the welfare and livelihood of the native tribes living in the desert, although some beasts, such as the elephant, rhinoceros, and giraffe, which were formerly found there, are now disappearing, having gone further north into better-watered districts.

Perhaps the most plentiful species of game found here is the springbok; their number runs into hundreds of thousands. They usually go in herds of fifty to a hundred. One resident told me that he had once seen about fifty thousand springbok pass his camp in twenty-four hours. Apparently they were on trek, seeking new pastures and water supplies.

In addition to springbok other game include hartebeest, tssessebe, duiker, stembok, kudu, wildebeest, and eland. It is remarkable the good condition wild game maintain living in such a thirst-land—all except the wildebeest, who often become lean and weak. When they are in this poor condition it is possible to walk up to an animal and just push it over.

Some years ago in the Kalahari there occurred a great migration of the springbok gazelle for which to-day we cannot account. The springbok is as natural to South Africa as the fox is to England, and was formerly found all over the sunny south. Now his range is restricted, and he has been driven further and further back. The springbok has a periodic migration, similar to the lemmings of Norway, which will cross mountains and rivers and are carried forward by an irresistible force, as yet undetermined. So with the springbok; and on this occasion they set out in hundreds of thousands. It began in the Transvaal, and the animals, collecting in herds, headed for the Kalahari.

They could not find sufficient water for their needs; they lapped up every ounce and went on, leaving the scattered dead. Vultures appeared in hundreds, for never had such a feast presented itself, and soon the bones of the dead littered the desert.

Still they went on, through the Kalahari, reaching the borders of what was known as German South-West Africa, where water is scarce. All that was left of this herd, which at the outset may have numbered half-a-million, surged onward until it reached the end, the sea. There the survivors drank of sea-water in despair and died, bleaching the shore with their skeletons. What impelled them to leave a land of plenty? We still search for the answer.

The springbok prefers the open spaces. High grass he does

not like : this conceals danger. Wild dogs can lie hidden in it, and lions can gain a near approach. The springbok, standing only about eighteen inches high at the shoulder, has no command of the ground. As he passes through the grass of the veld he goes with daintily picked and fearful footsteps. He is alert for even the slightest of noises. He will jump at his own shadow, and runs like one possessed when, over the top of the grass, something appears which he imagines to be an enemy, but is often merely a fellow springbok.

Concealed down-wind, I have watched these animals at night and noted how they come to water, especially when hidden in the grass and scrub, which may also contain a real foe. They approach hesitatingly, one wary animal taking the lead. The safety of the herd seems to be confided in him, and he halts every now and then. Perhaps he hears some noise that is unfamiliar ; there comes a sharp whistle from the scout, and the whole herd makes for the open. After a time, when they consider the threatening danger has gone, they get together once more . . . they almost gain the edge of the water-hole, when another alarm sounds, and they are off, helter-skelter. But thirst is compelling, and so they return yet again to the pool, where at last they drink hastily and retire, until the following night, when the process of dodging danger and death has to be repeated.

The various game have, however, one good friend and ally —the ostrich. We may think of this strange-looking bird as usually standing with its head buried in the sand, refusing to spot possible danger near it. This idea certainly does not apply correctly to the Kalahari, for there the ostrich takes on the task of spotting danger for a herd while it is resting. The game may well be hidden in the grass, and so is the ostrich ; but its long neck is raised just above it, rather like a periscope which is difficult to spot. Its ever-watchful eye can then detect an approaching enemy and give its animal friends timely warning.

Natives prefer ostrich meat to any other, although it is too strong and oily for a white man's palate. The eggs, however, are a different matter. They are palatable and very little different except in size from the ordinary English hen's. There are various ways of eating an ostrich egg, but this is one recipe :   a small hole is made in the top, a stick is inserted, and the inside

H 2

beaten up ; the egg is then broken open and its contents mixed with a pound of butter or lard, which, after cooking, makes a dish of buttered egg sufficient for from four to six hungry persons.

An ostrich has its senses highly developed, and to get within range of one demands care and caution. The Bushmen and Hottentots have their own methods of dealing with ostriches. They start by finding the spot where a hen ostrich is nesting, and then wait till she has laid her full complement of eggs. When satisfied on this point, the hunter hides within range of the nest. If he is a Bushman he carries his bow and arrow, and if a Hottentot he usually has his gun. Presently the hen bird takes up her position on the nest, and is shot and removed. The hunter then waits for the cock bird, who, not knowing of the fate of his mate, arrives to take his turn, and is dealt with in the same way, the eggs also being taken. The hunter eats the flesh of the bird and the inside of the egg, and keeps the sinews for making traps. The shells of the eggs supply water-bottles, and the feathers are often traded at a local store in exchange for tobacco or a cooking-pot. So that in the end no part of the ostrich is wasted.

The Government has issued proclamations that ostriches are not to be shot, but, as we have seen, laws and proclamations are hard to apply to Bushmen.

One of the peculiarities of game in the desert is that they accumulate in their paunches quantities of liquid. This may amount to as much as two gallons. This hidden reservoir is a bait to lions who, by killing an animal, get sufficient refreshment in the arid wastes and thus are saved long journeys to distant water-holes.

Even the lion, however, does not get his quarry without careful stalking. It may take him a day or more to get within killing range.

This is the scene. An antelope grazes quietly in a shady clearing. Unknown to him, the lion's vigil has been going on for hours. Suddenly the antelope lifts his head and with a twitch of his nostrils scents danger. Skilfully the lion moves forward up-wind, and with his doubts lulled by the silence and the absence of scent, the antelope returns to his grazing. But the lion creeps closer, until within springing range ; there is the snap of a twig, then a rush of ominous sound, and the antelope, thoroughly terrified, starts to run for his life. But it is too late; the lion lands cleanly on his back, and all is over.

I have seen antelopes standing statue-still and listening intently for long periods, wondering what the noise can be that comes from the thicket close by, moving an ear every now and again, a super-sensitive organ in this still air. Most antelopes hate the glare of the sun; they are true children of the jungle, and revel in the shade, where they lie up when not feeding.

The lion likewise can remain very still, hidden in the grass where he is able to conceal himself as his colour harmonizes with its usual burnt-up appearance. He lies stealthily watching your line of march, raising his head now and then to get a full view of the surroundings, and as quietly lowering it. He wants you to leave him alone—unless he is a man-eater.

To illustrate that the lion is not naturally aggressive towards humans we have only to visit the African National Reservations, such as the Kruger National Park in the Transvaal. There lions will stand within a few feet of you if you are in a motor-car and do nothing; should you, however, leave your car, then trouble might start; the lion will at once put himself on the defensive against possible attack.

There may be another reason for his good humour in these parks, for he seems to know instinctively that in them he is safe from man—or rather from his rifle or gun. This applies to most animals. In Kenya the game appear to realize where the unmarked boundary of their reserve runs. On the safe side they wander at will, but a few yards away on the wrong side are not to be seen, knowing they are once more hunted.

In the Kalahari Desert you must always be ready to meet a lion, and must never turn your back on him. When a lion does decide to attack and fight, he is determined to kill, and so it is your death or his. If he has been stung by a bullet he is the more infuriated, and this definitely means the death of one or the other, the hunter or the hunted. It matters not what wounds have been inflicted; in his rage to get at you he will carry all but a vital shot.

When a lion is really hungry he leaves no stone unturned to find food, and fear never enters into his calculations. When his appetite is satisfied it is another thing ; he does not want to fight or expose himself, but is ready for sleep, and sleeps heavily. He is one of the swiftest animals on earth over a hundred yards, and you have to reckon on reaching his brain, heart, or spine, in two or three seconds, which is all the time you have before he reaches you.

Natives dislike lions, for they usually have no firearms capable of immediate killing. If they do come on a lion in the veld their first thought and act is to bolt up the nearest tree. Sometimes the lion will go away, but, on the other hand, he may decide to wait. The native's only hope is that some of his friends may appear and chase the enemy away. This is all part of the fatalistic attitude of the native, which is a study in itself.

Have you ever heard a wild lion roar ? If so, you will know the difference between this and the whisper heard in a zoo. To hear ten of them roaring lustily, with two shot—first a big lioness, then a charging lion, with one hesitating whether to charge or not—is music and excitement ; the ground seems to quake.

Man and his rifle are the principal enemy of the lion, but the war-lord of the bush has another, of whom I have already spoken : a small and insignificant one—the porcupine ; it is, however, an adversary that in his very defeat and death wins the victory ; the lion seems to know it, and will only attack a porcupine if hard pressed and bordering on starvation.

In a battle between such a David and Goliath, the porcupine generally brings about the death of his assailant by sticking him full of quills with flail-like movements of the tail. Goliath is turned into a raging pin-cushion, with little possibility of ever removing the pins.

The porcupine, like the Londoner, always seems to be in a hurry. He has a large number of quills on back and tail, black spears edged with white at the ends, and varying in length from one to four inches. Hidden in his fur, of which they are a development, and lightly attached, these prickles have many barbs tucked away in the stem, each appearing immediately on contact with flesh. No other animal except the porcupine can so well teach the lion to mind his own business.

Over the rest of the desert and the bush he holds undisputed sway and his appearance sounds the tocsin of alarm. At his approach the antelopes become agitated, the jungle fowl seek safety in flight, and all the bird and animal world makes off in a flutter of colour.

A bad enemy of game in the Kalahari is the wild dog, known to most of us through Kipling's jungle stories. In packs of from six to a dozen, they run down their prey, tracking it in relays, another team of dogs taking over when the first has reached a certain point. There is no escape from these packs once they settle on the trail. The early morning, when the inhabitants of the desert search for food, is the wild dog's opportunity; the eland and other antelopes are the quarry.

The biggest and strongest dog leads the pack. He takes command and directs operations. They keep as far as possible to the grass, throwing a half-circle round the game, which may be three or four hundred yards away and usually in the open.

When all is ready, and they have come out into this open stretch, the leading dog shoots forward; the others have been watching him and follow, each in his appointed place. The dogs give out a series of savage, blood-curdling yaps; the quarry hears it and breaks into a panic-stricken gallop, going all out, with the fan-shaped red pack swiftly closing in.

Soon the antelope gets into his stride, and then we see why he has been called one of the fastest animals in the world. Other animals are away in flight, but the wild dogs keep on to their first target. Over the desert they seem to fly, heading towards their victim, dashing through patches of grass, bursting in and out of the scrub jungle, and all the time the distance between hunters and hunted slowly decreases. The hunt may go on for ten or fifteen miles, but the antelope is doomed; yet it struggles on, hoping that somehow it may escape alive.

Other dogs join the chase; it is all part of the wild dog organization. In the hunt the tired ones take a rest; then they go on more leisurely, taking no notice of other antelopes they may pass, even though within killing range; for by some strange law, they stick to the game originally marked down.

After a dozen miles, the pace of the antelope begins to slacken; its vitality and staying powers are giving way, and the intervening space is lessened until the leading dog is almost alongside . . .

he comes up with a rush . . . his fangs grip close on the under-side of the hunted animal. It is the end ; the rest of the pack surge in ; there is an overpowering chorus of savage yelps. The hunt is over : the dogs' feast has begun.

Leopards and hyenas are other enemies game have to face. The leopard—the " tiger " of Africa—is stealthy and cunning, and will often disappear as if by magic. He is fearless, savage, and vindictive, and when wounded will charge, even if a dozen rifles are blazing at him. He lives upon the smaller animals, and the domestic species, such as goats, sheep, donkeys, fowls, and dogs. He likes plenty of cover, and will lie flat along the branch of a tree, from which he springs at his prey, or at a hunter or native. If closely hunted he lies motionless, concealed in the grass, until his pursuers have passed. The early morning is usually the best time to find leopards on the prowl.

A wounded leopard is always dangerous, for he lies up so that any cover conceals him, and is ever ready to spring with lightning rapidity. He will maul and bite, and if there is more than one enemy or victim he springs from one to another in a matter of seconds. He never leaves a trail in the grass ; you may be approaching him without knowing it, when he is suddenly upon you.

The leopard is one of the most dangerous of the *carnivora*, being agile and having great vitality, and a daring and courage unequalled. Here I might say that a leopard's skin is so loose on its body that when it moves forward after being shot it covers the hole made by the bullet. Thus little blood is left behind to help in tracking it through the grass.

The leopard weighs about one hundred pounds and has four sets of talons which it uses to rip and disembowel its victims, and with which it can drag carcases twice its own weight into the fork of a tree several feet from the ground. This enables it to feed quietly and without interference from hyenas and jackals. The leopard, with the hyena, wild dog, and snake, has no friends amongst other animals ; nor have they protection under the game laws, being classed as dangerous vermin. Yet such is the working of Nature that these creatures tend to a consistent increase in numbers.

Giraffe and elephant are found in considerable numbers in

Portrait of a Bushman.

This is a copy of a Bushman cave painting. It is
remarkable that such a dynamic form of art should
belong to so primitive a people.

The life of the Bushmen, as we can see from this
photograph, has changed hardly at all since the
painting was executed, probably many centuries ago.

the northern part of the Bechuanaland Protectorate, but this is really outside the true desert area. The giraffe is, of course, a towering creature that lopes along in an extraordinary and fascinating way. It has no wish to harm either man or beast, and is highly-strung and nervous, and it is only under the galling conditions of captivity that he shows signs of temper; this is often with a kick of his hind-foot, like a sledge-hammer blow.

The giraffe is the only animal that is quite mute, and the only sound it makes is an occasional clicking when its cloven hoof strikes the ground. It sleeps standing up, is susceptible to chills, and when young has a delicate digestion. When a giraffe is shot for the pot it provides a luxury dish for the natives. How the Bushmen love a good fat giraffe! They never waste a particle. The marrow-bones are their particular delight, and I know myself what a tasty dish they are.

The chief reason why the elephant keeps away from the real desert country is that it is unable to find enough food there. There is no animal in the world which can equal the elephant's capacity for food. The ordinary African species requires about eight hundred pounds' weight per day, and it drinks a considerable quantity of water. As it is, even in good feeding areas it spends eighteen hours out of the twenty-four eating; and where there are many trees it spends much of its time breaking them down, merely to strip them of the small amount of foliage it gives.

The elephant hates the human voice, but has a greater dislike of fire. After the rains, when the jungle shoots up and the people of the desert reap their meagre crops, all sorts of schemes are adopted to scare away the elephants. Firebrands are scattered about and the jungle lighted. Sometimes, terrified by the sight and crackling of the fire, the elephants charge down on the fire-bearers, and finding that the danger is more apparent than real, they come to the conclusion that this may be a good way of living, and so we see the evolution of the rogue elephant who takes on the man-killing habit.

The wild animals of the Kalahari are not easy to find. By night and in the early dawn they make themselves heard. The lion and leopard prey on them all, prowling silently from cover to cover, well knowing how to make themselves invisible. They have need of invisibility, for their existence depends upon the ability to catch animals gifted with exceptional powers of sight, scent, and hearing. Unluckily for the lion he can himself be scented a long way off, so must approach the game up-wind. For quite lengthy periods the ground is exceptionally hard and dry, and however quietly the lion moves there is sure to be some dry leaf or twig that snaps and gives the warning.

It is impossible to over-estimate the acute hearing of wild animals until you have stalked them over dry leaves and through the sandy scrub desert. A leaf may drop from branch to branch and the antelope never starts ; but let there be ever so light a crackling of leaves under the foot of the hunter, and at once the animal knows something is happening. That is why, when out after game, it is vital to get on the leeward side.

The wild life of the Kalahari, although not easily found, abounds on every side. By night and in the early dawn the desert is full of sound. The lion, the leopard, the hyena, and the wild dog prey on them all, and, perhaps one should add, so does the Bushman.

Unfortunately these wonderful herds of wild animals are, for various reasons, decreasing. The vastness of the Kalahari makes policing difficult, and as a result poachers come in and slaughter numbers of game. The Administration has proclaimed 6,000 square miles in the north-east of the Territory as a Game Reserve ; in the southern part of the Kalahari the Union Government has set aside a million acres to form the Kalahari National Park, where wild life will be completely protected and given a sense of security. This will also preserve for future generations the interesting fauna that exists there to-day, which otherwise would soon disappear.

OF SNAKES AND SUCHLIKE

IN addition to the larger game with which the Kalahari Desert abounds, the country supports smaller mammalia such as meercats, rock rabbits, spring-hares, hares, antbears, baboons, lemurs, rats, mice, and bats. Where there are rats and mice there are snakes, and the desert swarms with them. They range from small tree-snakes to pythons from twelve to fifteen feet in length.

The only creatures never troubled by the lack of water are the snakes, of which Africa's most deadly is the black mamba. I remember once riding behind a companion when we came across one of these creeping murderers. It appeared right in our path, and with head raised about four feet from the ground was stabbing its fangs in our direction. My fearless friend rode straight at it and gave the snake a blow over the head with his carbine, from which it recoiled . . . and we galloped on.

One night, after supper, I leaned back to take it easy against my propped-up saddle. Suddenly I became aware of something heavy slithering across my legs ; petrified as any desert stone I remained perfectly still, whilst Africa's deadliest snake passed on its course like an evil dream. Had I moved, and so aroused its enmity, these words would never have been written.

Brief mention should be made here of the Nogapotsane—a strange animal unknown to zoos, but which the natives of the Kalahari assert exists. Many of them, indeed, say they have seen this legendary beast.

The first record of its appearance is about sixty years ago. A man came upon the snake—for that is its form—coiled up, but could not see its head. As he watched, it straightened itself and moved forward, dislodging large stones as it moved. " The noise of its movement was like that of a wagon passing over stony ground."

The man ran to his chief with the story. Trackers were sent out to kill the beast, and although the reptile by this time had disappeared, its spoor was still visible.

The Nogapotsane is reputed to be from twenty-five to forty feet in length, and very thick. Many natives say that it carries a short horn in the centre of its forehead. It has four stumps on the underside of its body, which are supposed to be rudimentary legs. The head is like that of a snake, but has " more of a face ", as the natives describe it. The nose is equipped with nostrils, from which comes death-dealing smoke. Even when emitting this, the snake is able to create a cold wind. This wind is a feature of all eye-witness stories. Its cry is like that of a goat.

The natives hold that the Nogapotsane is a supernatural animal, which has the power to make people faint ; after which, if they recover, they crawl about on their faces for indefinite periods. Others say it is an ominous sign, only appearing to those about to die, although its cry carries no danger or evil omen.

There is no reason why some strange, rare animal such as this should not exist in the Kalahari, and it is possible that a large, horned, python-like creature does live there. It will be an exciting day for any zoo when it is able to exhibit this fantastic animal.

One reason why the Kalahari has not been developed is the tsetse fly, which has for centuries been bringing sleeping sickness to human beings and death to horses and cattle.

This brown, deadly insect about the size of a house-fly, active by day but quiet by night, bars large parts of Africa to Europeans, and rinderpest, through the tsetse fly, ravages the herds. The fly, like the mosquito, prefers to be near water. So it preys on wild life, but has no effect upon the thick-skinned elephant, nor does the giraffe seem to suffer. The mosquito has its low humming note, quite distinct from other winged pests, and the tsetse fly has an indescribable buzz, a note to itself. When you hear it you know there is death in the air for horses, oxen, and dogs, and, unless antidotes are nearby, a living death for man.

When a mosquito bites, you know all about it. Not so with the tsetse. Nor does it make cattle kick and switch their tails as happens when a gadfly is operating. This is part of the secret armament of the tsetse and the silent and insidious way he has of bringing death. With animals there are no immediate symptoms, but after a day or two the eyes and nose begin to water. This is the fatal sign, this is the beginning ; then the jaws swell up, the animal loses appetite, and it can only recline in a state of collapse, unable to get up and graze ; gradually it dies from exhaustion.

Donkeys and goats are immune from the tsetse, but as the donkey and the goat are of little general use in the desert, this does not help matters much.

Butterflies and moths are plentiful in the Kalahari, some of them having beautiful colouring.   White ants are a great plague, as they are in many parts of Africa.   Their hills are found all over the desert, sometimes of considerable size.   They are destructive, eating everything in a house or hut that is not made of metal.   The Bushmen are fond of one species of ant which is known as " Bushman's rice ".

One might imagine that vegetation is scarce here, yet after the infrequent rains there is a surprising growth.   All kinds of plants blush pink and purple in the sunlight.   There is even a delicate maidenhair fern, a delight to the botanist.   But the prize is the wild melon which seems to have been invented by Nature as an antidote to the drought of the Kalahari.

After good rains this melon appears in the form of a tuber, twelve inches below ground.   It looks like a large bottle, and inside is a cool liquid.   Elephants are particularly fond of it and dig it out with a gardener's skill and care.

Another plant with a cool and tasty liquid is a creeper with tentacles from a circular root.   Animals, as well as man, know how to tap the supply by scratching down a few inches.   Another creeper, known as *mokuri*, has tubers as big as a football, growing outwards horizontally from the stem in a circle of three or four feet.   The Bushman sharpens a stick, thrusts it through a stone, pushes the stick in the ground, and with the stone as fulcrum levers up the tuberous roots to the surface.

IRRIGATION AND THE FUTURE

WHAT does the future hold for the Kalahari ?
We have seen it as an arid waste-land, a thirst-land,
where if only there were water. . . .

Water—that is the one essential thing which could change this
desert into a land that might have considerable value to human
beings and civilization.

Not so long ago—a hundred years—water in the Kalahari
came mainly from Lake Ngami. It was Livingstone who first
saw this lake, " this fine-looking sheet of water. . . . We could
detect no horizon." It took him three or four days to go round
it ; now it is only an expanse of reeds, with here and there a patch
of muddy water. By sinking wells, however, there is proof that
water could be made available.

Livingstone came from the south, and, as he says, passed
through a flat country covered with open forest, bush, and an
abundance of grass. To a certain extent he was lucky in his
observations, for it is now known that the previous rainy season
had been a record one. The trees were of the acacia variety, the
soil sandy, and there were wells and cattle stations—now no
more.

Farther north he came across a sort of fountain, and a mimosa
with lilac-like flowers. Then for seventy or eighty miles no
water was to be found. At one point his party came to a stratum
of sand below ground level. This was a remarkable find, and
when it was dug through the water flowed away and the water-
hole at once became empty. It disappeared down into the earth
and gave proof that it could be brought out by artificial means.
At the present time water required at water-points on the railway
line is brought up from a depth of 2,000 feet.

Farther on, Livingstone had evidence of shell-fish living in
the Kalahari ; this seemed to indicate that the desert must once
have been part of a large inland sea.

Salt pans, fifteen or twenty miles round, covered with lime
deposits, barred their route. Here were strange mirages : " The

mirage on these salinas was marvellous," wrote Livingstone. "Here no imagination was necessary for realizing the exact picture of large collections of water. The waves danced along the surface, and the shadows of the trees were vividly reflected in such an admirable manner that the loose cattle, whose thirst had not been slaked by the very brackish water of Nchokotsa, with the horses, dogs, and even the Hottentots, ran off towards the deceitful pools. A herd of zebras in the mirage looked exactly like elephants. Then a sort of break in the haze dispelled the illusion."

Water! If only water could reappear the Kalahari might become in the future an agricultural and pastoral country. There are schemes of irrigation which have great possibilities. Long ago the northern part of the Protectorate was watered from streams flowing into it. It was then full of animal and vegetable life—almost a paradise.

Strange are the workings of nature! While all appeared to be going well, suddenly the wells of abundance dried up. Through a geological accident, for which to-day we cannot account, the Malopo and other rivers flowing into, and through, the Kalahari, were diverted to the Zambezi, a river that often overflowed its banks and therefore had no need of any additional water to keep it in motion. This increased volume swept on through the Zambesi basin, and what is now Rhodesia and Portuguese East Africa, to the Indian Ocean, there to empty itself into the sea— the waters that could have made of the Kalahari a wonderland of production. Lakes and depressions, also, to a large extent, dried up ; year by year the water-level sank lower and lower.

In the past eighty years this decrease in the water-level has created another problem, as it is doing elsewhere in Africa. Formerly wells sunk a few feet into the ground produced water in varying quantities, but now one has to go down far deeper, hundreds and even thousands of feet below the ground surface. Geological conditions are obviously undergoing variation in the Kalahari, and it is a task for scientists to retrieve the waters and divert them into their former channels, thus perhaps opening up millions of acres for the extensive production of cattle, grain, and fruit.

To appreciate the possibilities of the Kalahari for stock-raising and food-production, we must have a clear idea of its geographical setting. We know that the greatest extent lies within the Bechuanaland Protectorate, and we will now examine the river systems by which irrigation might be carried out.

On the north-west border of the desert is the Portuguese colony of Angola ; in the highlands rise three large rivers, all flowing to the south-east. These are the Zambezi, Linyanti, and Okavango, all three running parallel with each other and turning eastward within, and adjacent to, the Kalahari.

The Okavango becomes lost in the swamps which fringe the desert's northern border ; the water sinks into the earth or disappears by evaporation ; only the underground flow eventually finds its way, greatly reduced in volume, to the Makarikari depression in the central Kalahari where it comes up in springs. Steps are now being taken to open up the channels of the Okavango and utilize the water flowing into the swamps. If this can be done, and the papyrus and other reeds cleared away, it will bring a great flow of water into Lake Ngami.

Like the Okavango, the Linyanti also divides into a mass of swamps which link up with and join the Zambezi in its course to the Indian Ocean. We see that most of the water is lost in these swamps: evaporation absorbs a large quantity, while transpiration in the swamps takes much of it. The fact that the water flows underground towards some central depression in the Kalahari where it can find no exit, is of profound interest and importance in solving the problem of water supply.

In 1920 Professor Schwarz of Cape Colony gave the opinion that the water of the Linyanti, by some processs of nature, had been diverted to the Zambezi, where, he declared, it flowed on southwards into Lake Ngami and points to the east of the lake. This deviation by Nature, if it happened, must have occurred in bygone ages, for, as we have seen, when Livingstone saw the lake it was after an exceptional rainfall and it really differed little from what it does to-day.

True, there is a certain amount of evidence to support Schwarz's theory in the present normal quantity of water in the Ngami, and other erstwhile lakes, which may have been inland seas, and of this we have the assertions of travellers who preceded Livingstone.

Schwarz maintained that the diversion of the Linyanti was the cause of the trouble, and that if it could be turned back and made to flow along its old-time course, all would be well. His scheme involved the complete reclamation of the Okavango marshes, their division into canals, and a system of dams and waterways on a large scale. He visualized the waters spreading out over the Kalahari, bringing hundreds of thousands of acres under cultivation, and so converting it into a land of milk and honey.

Schwarz's statements created much argument; meteorologists and scientists of all grades came into the discussion, and there is no doubt that he raised a problem affecting also other desert areas, such as the Tarim Desert in Chinese Turkistan, where the waters of the Tarim become lost like the Linyanti and create exactly the same irrigation problem.

Despite the energy of his campaign, Schwarz's theory was generally discredited, but the problem still awaits solution.

In the able report presented to the South African Government by Senator A. M. Conroy in 1946, to which I shall again allude, many of Schwarz's inaccuracies and contradictions were described as being based on insufficient knowledge. Credit should, however, be given to him for having maintained interest in the potentialities of the Kalahari. Although many of Schwarz's expectations are incapable of fulfilment, other possibilities arising out of investigation of his theories may one day be brought to fruition. He blazed the trail to development and production in what one day may be a miniature Nile Valley.

In 1924 a survey party was sent out to investigate the Schwarz theory; they sifted all the evidence on the spot, and came to the conclusion that the Linyanti had not been diverted within historical times, whatever may have happened in the distant past. The waters of the rivers were lost in the swamps and had nothing to do with any attraction towards the Zambezi. The surveyors considered that the Okavango River could be made to provide quantities of water through a system of canals, but it would involve a large expenditure of money, time, and labour. They could find no evidence that Lake Ngami had ever been an inland sea, nor could they agree that the climate had deteriorated in historical times, and decided that there is no possibility of improvement by the creation of inland seas.

On one angle of this vital question the survey party agreed : they considered that if the swamps of the Okavango could be canalized, and a dam built on the Zambezi at its junction with the swamps of the Linyanti, there were possibilities for the irrigation of that part of the Kalahari.

In August, 1945, the Conroy Expedition finished their survey of the water systems, and reached the conclusion that development is possible in certain areas, and that the waters of the rivers lost in the swamps and marshes, or flowing on unused into the Indian Ocean, could be utilized and made to provide increasing sections for food production. I shall deal with their recommendations later on.

The Times, in a recent leading article, said :

The general conclusions of the engineers in the party are very similar to those of the reconnaissance survey of 1924. They believe that if the swamps are canalized—a work which they do not think will be ruinously expensive—it will be possible to irrigate important areas of Bechuanaland, and provide waterways which would be a boon to the natives who live in the area and now have only earth tracks for transport. Even if the irrigation is ruled out, as it may be, by the unsuitability of the irrigable soil, the provision of water in good ranching veld, whose only present drawback is that it lacks watering points for stock, might still be worth while. What has now been established is that there are most attractive possibilities in the northern Kalahari for waterway and agricultural development, if not for rain-making. And it is almost certain that these possibilities will at last be studied in the only satisfactory way— by a detailed survey carried out by a properly equipped expedition.

It is here in the Kalahari that one of the problems of Africa is challenging human ingenuity, where man is fighting both the water and the tsetse menace.

Parts of the Kalahari and Bechuanaland in general may in time become a land of plenty, dotted here and there with groups of trees planted by Nature and man. The coming of an adequate water supply would make certain areas of the land habitable and green, a land reminiscent of that which Livingstone knew, before the waters receded once more. In the transition it is to be hoped that the Bushman will be saved, for he is of great interest to the ethnologist and the antiquarian ; and these primitive humans should be preserved as the earliest link with prehistoric man.

A pleasing feature of the Kalahari is the national park in the south, an area set aside for the preservation of the graceful gemsbok, and many other antelopes, as well as lions, zebras, and giraffes. Its eighteen hundred square miles of unfenced ground offer fascinating sights, where wild life can be seen moving in its natural haunts. Thanks to the South African Government this wild life will be viewed without risk, and a practical knowledge of the habits of big game is made available. The hardships and dangers of former times will be exchanged for comfort and security ; the lion, the giraffe, and the zebra may be seen from the motor-car, which, to a lion, appears no more dangerous than a large moving log, for the lion is never inconvenienced by not having the plastic, stereoscopic qualities of the human sight. A car can be opened or closed ; those sitting in it merely figure in the upper row of outlines, and are never taken by the lion as its enemies.

Moreover, when travelling through this game preserve of the Kalahari, you can wear what coloured clothes you like, for lions are almost colour-blind, and no matter how gaudy your raiment it will never irritate them. Then, again, in spite of a highly developed sense of hearing in lions, the normal human voice is of no interest to them. Noises which refer to the prey they are stalking, or their love-making and social and fighting instincts, alone hold their attention.

If the plans for this immense Whipsnade are brought to fruition, the visitor will be able to make close acquaintance with the wild life of the Kalahari.

What are the other possibilities of the desert in the near future ?

As already remarked, Senator A. M. Conroy of the South African Government carried out an exploratory survey of the Kalahari towards the end of 1945, and his report on its future makes illuminating reading.

It says, of course, that the limiting factor to development is the lack of water. There are indications that in many places there is little or no annual accretion to the underground waters from rainfall, and that the slight amount of ground water is soon exhausted by pumping. Boreholes have, from time to time, been sunk at various likely places, of which some were fairly good, others contained brine, and some were dry.

As the report says, it is apparent that large tracts of the Kalahari are incapable of being transformed into gardens of luscious growth. Indeed, to enable these regions to support stock on a ranching basis, it would be essential to provide, at intervals of not more than five or six miles, a system of boreholes or reservoirs supplied from artificial catchments, on the lines used by the Romans in the western desert of Egypt. When they crossed the Mediterranean, more than two thousand years ago, to develop pastures and granaries for Southern Europe, the Romans must have found a land similar to the Kalahari. The most practical engineers of their day, they overcame the difficulties by cutting subterranean cisterns in the limestone and building contour walls to lead the run-off from the rainfall to the cisterns. The small size—two-and-a-half feet—of the mouth of the cistern compared with the underground excavation, about twenty-five feet square by twenty deep, retarded the normal high evaporation. Curiously enough, during the North African campaign of the Second World War, these watering places, still operating successfully, were, after being cleaned out, utilized by the Allied armies.

Senator Conroy states that, fundamentally, the problem is how to make the best use of an average annual rainfall of seven to nineteen inches, which rapidly evaporates. Nature has overcome this problem to a marked degree in her clothing of the Kalahari with its present vegetal cover, which adequately supports the wild life inhabiting the region. The presence of man and his domestic animals in any concentration in these parts, especially without the strictest control, can only serve to upset the balance of Nature and transform the country into a barren waste.

Senator Conroy adds that " those who fear ' the spread of the Kalahari ' may be assured that this is likely to follow only from man's occupation of the area, but if left to Nature this region is just as likely to improve."

Further investigation is necessary before any vital decisions can be taken. It is important to stress that a large-scale development utilizing the river waters must await the result of the investigation of many factors. This, however, does not mean that certain irrigation plants, local waterways, and the distribution of water from the swamps towards ranching areas for stock watering and so on, may not be developed on a small scale in accordance with an interim plan based on more rapid reconnaissance.

Possession of valuable resources avails little, says Senator Conroy, if rail and highway communications are lacking. Although internal communication by water is possible in some parts of the Kalahari, full-scale development of its resources can follow only after the construction of extensive railways, the feasibility of which would depend upon many economic factors and a measure of co-operation between the various administrations concerned. " The area is vast and the potentialities are great. With a large section of the world's population facing starvation, economy may to a certain extent have to be subordinated to expediency."

PART THREE

THE GOBI DESERT

For over two thousand years the Great Wall of China, shown here and over the page, has grandly stood the tests of time.

The builders of the Great Wall
overcame obstacles which would
have defeated lesser men.

A HUNDRED MILLION YEARS AGO

LEAST known and most inaccessible to Europeans of all the great deserts of the world is the Gobi—or Shamo, as the Chinese call it—of Central Asia. Here in this realm of deserts and mountains one meets with evidence of a marvellous past. Our curiosity is aroused by the relics that have been discovered of Neanderthal man, who lived and died here thousands of years ago. The most ancient remains of primitive man have been found near by, the antiquity of which is estimated to be approximately a million years.

Our imagination turns to those men of the past who had a passion to overcome the seemingly impossible—Genghiz Khan, the Mongol conqueror, Tamerlane " the Magnificent ", Marco Polo, that remarkable traveller of the Middle Ages, and many others.

Yet there still remains to-day much magic charm in these desert spaces, where modern civilization has made few inroads, and pilgrims find time to visit the monasteries with their lamas or priests engaged in a lifetime of prayer.

The Gobi, a name which means " the Great Desert ", forms a large depression between the Tibetan highlands in the south and Siberia in the north and west, where the Altai Mountains, once the private property of the Tsar, enclose it. Along the eastern edge is Manchuria. Twelve hundred miles across, six hundred from north to south, and in places five thousand feet above sea-level, it is one of the world's desolate areas. The east is mainly sand and sand dunes, but the central and western sections are covered with grass, thorn bush, and scrub, with a soil in places that looks as if it would grow anything.

Like all deserts, water is the main problem and difficulty for the Mongolian tribes scattered throughout the Gobi. In the east it is found only at wells and is alkaline in taste. In the west are rivers and lakes that could make it a wonderful country for agriculture and the raising of cattle and sheep. Throughout its length the desert is crossed by three main caravan routes, the first from Kalgan and the Great Wall to Kyakhta, the second and central one from Kansu, and the westerly one from Chinese Turkistan at Hami.

With the exception of the western caravan route, water is found only in wells at varying intervals and is usually brackish.

Along the eastern road the camel has to a large extent been displaced by the motor-car, but for the carriage of heavy merchandise he still plods his way from well to well. Horses and yaks, the Tibetan oxen, are also used for transport purposes.

Here the camel is king; yet long ago this desert held the largest animal in the world. In the heart of the Gobi, on the line of the central caravan route, lived a number of prehistoric creatures known as dinosaurs. They have long since vanished, and scientists tell us they lived more than a hundred million years ago, a length of time that overpowers the imagination. The period was known as the Mesozoic Age, the Age of Reptiles that lived in a hot-house atmosphere, with no cold or frosts. Eggs and remains of the dinosaurs have been found principally in the Gobi Desert. It also harboured huge land animals, one of which exceeded in size any other land animal that has ever lived. The dinosaurs were carnivorous. Petrified eggs have been found exactly as they were left by the reptile, covered with sand, to be hatched out by the rays of the sun, a hundred million years ago !

Succeeding ice and glacial ages killed off the dinosaurs, and the nearest approach to them would be the dragons of Komodo Island in the Dutch East Indies. These, however, are tiny compared with the dinosaur, being not more than ten or twelve feet long. They appeared some twenty or thirty million years after the dinosaurs, but, like them, they are carnivorous and attack their food as the meat-eating dinosaurs did, tearing it off in great chunks, swallowing legs and shoulders whole, bones and all.

THE GREAT WALL OF CHINA

PART of the southern boundary of the Gobi is China's marvel—the Great Wall. Astronomers tell us that the only man-made thing on earth that could be seen from the moon is the Great Wall of China. This immense structure stretches from the shores of the Yellow Sea along the edge of the desert to Shahukow, where it trends south-west, to terminate on the borders of Kansu, a distance of nineteen hundred miles.

History rates the Great Wall as the Eighth Wonder of the World; it has certainly survived the other wonders, except the Great Pyramid. All the rest have faded out: the Hanging Gardens of Babylon, of which I could find no trace whatever; only a few columns remain of the Temple of Diana at Ephesus, while Jupiter Olympus of Phidias has entirely gone. The fine brass Colossus of Rhodes was capsized by an earthquake and robbers in the desert carried the pieces away . . . none knows where.

The Great Wall served a useful purpose in the days of bows and arrows, when artillery and siege trains were unknown, and kept out the invaders from the north and west; whereas the rest of the monuments were merely " preposterous edifices of exaggerated hugeness, of dazzling and ruinous luxury ".

Unfortunately for the creator of the wall, he never reaped the fame that was his due, for the Chinese eliminated him from history as an eternal punishment for having burned the ancient classics and buried alive five hundred learned men when they had the temerity to upbraid him for taking the title of the " First Emperor ". The burning of the classics appalled the *literati*, for anything with the stamp of age on it is revered in China.

The Great Wall was the barrier against an advance from the north; it covered Peking; and the steppe that extended from the Russian town of Kyakhta, south of Irkutsk in Siberia, for eight hundred miles to the wall, must be traversed by an invading army, and at the end of it they would have to tackle this military obstacle, which is a monument to Chinese tenacity and patience.

As the desert and the wall are closely related from their geographical, political, and strategical aspects, it is interesting to give its fascinating story. It came into being in this way.

In 219 B.C. there reigned in China one Tsin Shih Hwang Ti. The devastating raids of the nomad Huns had extended to China, and as a safeguard against their inroads the emperor decided to build a wall along the northern side of his empire, and so keep out an enemy he was unable to subdue in open fight. The idea of such an enterprise might well have appalled any man, but Shih Hwang Ti knew what he wanted, and meant to get it.

The story goes that he took a map, drew a line from Shan-hai-kwan on the Yellow Sea; 185 miles east of Peking, right across China almost to the borders of my consular district of Chinese Turkistan; and said; " Let there be a wall."

Having settled this important preliminary, he next took in hand the ways and means by which the wall should become an accomplished fact. It would cross ranges of high mountains, traverse deep valleys, run along the edge of the barren and desolate Gobi, and overcome every form of natural obstacle. Shih Hwang Ti never hesitated. He allocated an army of a quarter-of-a-million men, brought out all the prisoners of war and every civil criminal he could lay hands on, and transported whole tribes from different parts of China. He now parcelled out the wall into sections and posted the labour parties at selected intervals along the line of the proposed structure. To supply this army of workers the emperor mobilized the resources of his empire, establishing depots over the two thousand miles of wall. To these points food for the workers was transported, together with all the requisite tools, and when all were lined up the order to " go to it " was given.

The men and animals required for the delivery of this paraphernalia must alone have reached an enormous total, apart from the workers themselves, but no figures of the actual numbers exist. The old Chinese writings, however, record that approximately only one load in every fifty arrived at its destination, the rest being required for consumption on the way, or having otherwise disappeared, as things did in those days, and still do, in China, through bribery and corruption.

The Chinese are an eminently practical race, and wherever

possible the land was turned to good account; seed was sown, and in the fullness of time the crops were gathered in, and gradually the host of men and women were made self-supporting. This procedure brought more ground under cultivation, and reclaimed a certain amount of the Gobi territory; altogether the idea throws a sidelight on the vision and patience characteristic of the Chinese, and really explains why they were successful in overcoming the obstacles confronting them.

The workers having been distributed throughout the line, supplies organized, and other arrangements completed, the construction went on apace, and in fifteen years the wall was finished. History has no parallel with this amazing accomplishment, either in the amount of brick and stone used in its construction or in the sum of human labour expended upon it.

From time to time the wall has been repaired by successive dynasties, and even after the lapse of nearly twenty centuries it is still in a wonderful state of preservation, especially along the Gobi border. The dimensions vary with the sector; in the part with which we are concerned it is about twenty-five feet in height, twenty-five feet thick at the base, and fifteen feet wide along the top. The sides are of brick or stone, solidly buttressed, the inside being filled with brick and stone and earth well beaten down.

For long distances it is possible to drive a carriage and pair along the top, and in parts of the Gobi section two carriages could be taken abreast. Throughout its entire length the wall had more than eighteen thousand towers, each of which was a miniature fortress, and at every commanding point a signal beacon was erected so that in the event of an attack on any particular section of the wall reinforcements could be rushed there.

In order to provide for an efficient garrison, some of the tribes imported to the scene of operations were given inducements to settle permanently, whilst a proportion of trained soldiery were granted land and other facilities, so that a nucleus of regulars leavened the general mass.

Let us follow the wall over the Gobi section of it, from the point at Shan-hai-kwan where it starts from the sea, rising sheer from the water's edge. Soon after leaving there it quits the plains and ascends steadily towards the mountains for a distance of three hundred miles, until it attains an altitude of five thousand feet. The scenery over this area is magnificent, but for long distances there is no sign of life, apart from that of occasional birds, only a panorama and the silence characteristic of such regions.

In places the wall reaches a comparatively high altitude, and it is then that the immensity of the work becomes apparent—the dizzy heights over which it climbs, the sheer precipices to which it clings, where at some points it is actually necessary to climb with the aid of ropes. I was struck with amazement at the idea of building a wall in such inaccessible places ; the mind boggles at the amount of labour required for the cartage of the bricks and stone and for the transporting of food and water, and at the physical obstacles that were overcome in obedience to the will of one man.

All along this section the general state of preservation is excellent. Several passes are crossed, notably the Nankow Pass, one of the vital spots in the wall, down which swept many would-be raiders of the realm, to be checked and thrown back by the solid barrier they encountered. Because the need of a garrison here was recognized long after the wall and towers to the far west had ceased to serve any practical purpose, and had fallen into dilapidation, the Nankow section was frequently repaired and the defensive wall strengthened by a special system of fortifications.

Here it held in check the famous leader Genghiz Khan in the thirteenth century, although he, ultimately and after fierce fighting, pierced it at another point.

The Nankow Pass is one of the gateways to China from the north, and all travellers and convoys coming over the Gobi southwards pass through it. Beyond where the wall trends to the south-west and leaves the area in which we are interested, it becomes in parts only a rampart of earth and stones, with crumbling towers at intervals. In the thirteenth century it was the main line of defence against the Mongols, who were then a living force, but early in the fifteenth century they had ceased to be a menace.

Incidentally, we might well ask, what is the military value of the wall? In the days of bows and arrows, when the invading hordes were ill-equipped and unprovided with the means to demolish obstacles of this nature, it was an effective barrier and kept the barbarous tribes of the north from pouring into China, always a great attraction as the granary of Asia and offering unlimited opportunities for loot.

Against great leaders, controlling large and mobile armies such as those of Genghiz Khan, the wall did not prove an insurmountable obstacle, and throughout the eighteen centuries of its existence it has been frequently pierced, notably in 1644 by the Manchus, who for thirty years had tried to do so, and in the end succeeded. Notwithstanding its gradual decay and the decline of its glory, the Great Wall will remain a supreme and unique monument to Chinese genius.

§

THE MONGOLS

WHEN we hear the name Mongolia we picture to ourselves nothing but desert—a desert from which there came many centuries ago the vast army of horsemen that overran the western and eastern worlds, from the China Sea to Moscow and from Siberia to Delhi, whose leaders were such men as Genghiz Khan, Kublai Khan, and Tamerlane. The clouds of cavalry exist to-day in the herdsmen of the plains—Mongolia does not consist solely of desert; there are forests and rivers and lakes, with fertile stretches of pasture land. It is one of the few countries left where there is scope for the explorer, for many parts are still little known to the outside world.

In 1915 Mongolia threw off Chinese sovereignty. By the Treaty of Kyakhta, a town in Siberian territory on the north side of the Gobi, the country was recognized as an autonomous republic. Later there followed an alliance with Soviet Russia. The country was now divided into two parts, Outer Mongolia being a republic closely allied to the Soviet, and really under its domination, and Inner Mongolia being absorbed into China, although the dominion which this latter country exercised was loose and shadowy.

It is not easy to estimate the population of Mongolia—a good calculation would place the figure around four millions. These people are nomads, constantly on the move, looking for fresh pastures.

As nomads the Mongols have no fixed homes. They live in felt tents, or auls, peculiar to the tribes of Central Asia. These are warm and comfortable inside, being made of felt or skins fixed on a circular wooden framework, with an opening at the top to let out smoke from the fire lighted in the centre. The inside is carpeted with rugs, and in the case of wealthy Mongols is hung with embroidered cloths and coverings. Some of these tents are of considerable size. I have seen them as much as thirty feet across, with the floor strewn with beautiful rugs, and the finest silk hangings and tapestries along the sides. The chief and only drawback to an otherwise pleasing interior is the smoke from the argol, or camel-dung fuel. This gives out a pungent smell, gets into one's eyes, and makes them smart for hours afterwards. The Mongols, of course, are acclimatized to this unpleasantness.

In the larger auls there is always in front of the entrance, as you go in, a small altar with a statue of Buddha, flanked by prayer-wheels, which the devout turn as they enter and so ensure, they believe, their salvation.

The prayer-wheel is a fascinating instrument. It varies in size from the miniature that can be carried in a child's hand to the giant specimens found in Burma and Japan. Many of these are as high as a lofty room, one of them in Kyoto in Japan having within its interior 108 lamps, each a gem in workmanship. Some of the prayer-wheels I have seen in Mongolia were arranged like huge beer barrels on end, and held up to a million copies of the magic text :

> *Om ! ma-ni pad-me hu-ng.*
> (Hail ! jewel in the lotus flower.)

Far back in the mists of antiquity it was considered supremely beneficial for this super-spell to revolve before the eyes ; it was

The framework of an aul looks flimsy enough, but the finished article is built to withstand the Gobi winter.

A Buddhist monastery perched high among
the mountains of the Gobi.

unnecessary to utter it to secure its efficacy. Merely looking at it in its written form revolving on the wheel was considered to be of great spiritual value. Three of the basic ideas in this soothing and contemplative Buddhist faith were deliverance from earthly danger, the attainment of Nirvana (Paradise), and escape from hell. All these advantages could be secured through the magic spell, when constantly turned before the eyes. The prayer-wheel could perform these endless revolutions, and the greater the number of turns the higher the spiritual reward. So the prayer-wheel supplies a fervent spiritual need.

Over the central fireplace is a copper cauldron full of a dirty cream-coloured liquid, simmering constantly over the argol fire. This is the stock Mongolian dish and one of which they never tire. It is hard for the stranger to recognize it as tea—rancid-buttered tea ; a curious mixture, for which the taste is an acquired one. Apart from its peculiar preparation, even the tea itself seems different from the commodity we are accustomed to use. In Mongolia it is bought and sold in the form of tea-bricks. These bricks measure fifteen inches by ten inches and one inch deep ; they are compressed hard, and to use the tea a sharp knife pares off pieces, as in whittling a stick. The preparation of these bricks involves the actual tea-leaves' being first ground into a paste, mixed with a binding material, and then pressed into the standard size. Tea-bricks are also used as a form of currency ; thus half-a-dozen bricks might buy one sheep.

There are other shocks for the unsophisticated traveller. Like the Bushmen of the Kalahari, these nomads will eat almost anything. I once came across a party of them who had been having a picnic after some religious ceremonies. They were indulging in singing, drinking, and general jollification, and in their midst was something that looked to me like a large joint of meat.

" What is that ? " I asked in surprise.

" It's a leg of mutton," one of the Mongolians replied. " It belonged to my father." And he drew himself up with pride.

Dried meat, and especially mutton, is regarded as a special dish in the Gobi and is preserved as a family heirloom. With any luck it may last for years and grace many a banquet, since it is always given as a mark of honour to the chief guest. At the same time, however, it would be a grave breach of good manners to sample the offering, which is then left in the possession of its original owner.

On entering a Mongol tent snuff is invariably offered, and a few pinches of it are taken before opening up a conversation. Beautifully painted snuff-bottles are the hallmark of Mongol gentility; some of them are of gold and jade and encrusted with precious stones. No Mongol is ever without his or her snuff-bottle.

Apart from being voracious eaters, the Mongols have few vices. Sometimes they get intoxicated through drinking kumis, fermented mare's milk, from leathern bottles.

Dirt is their besetting sin, for they never wash, except under the sternest necessity, from the day they are born until the day they die. Indeed, their skin, which is normally of a rufous hue, becomes as black as the face of a London chimney-sweep. Their bodies they smear with butter to keep out the cold and to soften the wrinkling effect of the bitter winds; thus there are constantly accruing fresh protections when the grease comes in contact with the outside world. Yet the Mongols rarely grow fat.

The Mongol costume is difficult to define. It is really a kind of loose dressing-gown of common cloth or silk, lined with wool, reaching down to the knees and secured at the waist by a belt. Beneath this is a pair of wool-lined trousers, very baggy, which are stuffed into leather riding boots. For a hat the Mongol has a broad-brimmed felt affair that looks like an inverted saucer, with streamer ribbons hanging from the back and flying in the wind when the wearer is galloping over the desert.

The women dress in much the same way as the men, except that they do not wear a belt; in fact, the name for a woman in the Mongol language is " the unbelted one ", so there can be no doubt about it. Although men and women appear so much alike, you can tell the difference between them by the head-dress of the women, which is covered with silver and copper ornaments, as well as red and blue stones, although the shape of the hat is the same as the men's.

Both men and women use their riding boots as receptacles for various things, from spoons and forks to brick tea. Pipe and tobacco, and even drinking bowls, find a safe resting-place there.

The amount worn underneath depends upon the period of the year. As the winter advances so successive layers are added, since they have to allow for varying degrees of temperature.

Like other women the world over, the Mongol lady dresses her hair ; but she does so only once in every eight or ten weeks, and she keeps it in the correct position by plastering it with a kind of glue. She then plaits it on a flat framework curved outward like the horns of a sheep, these terminating in a silver plaque covered with beads and ornaments. She has earrings of turquoise and stones, and the wealthy add strings of beads and necklaces. Altogether the Mongol dress is a study for an artist.

In Mongolia there is no education as we know it. They train themselves to ride, fight, hunt, and look after sheep and cattle. They have a love of forest, mountain, and desert, and a knowledge of animals, and are excellent camp-fire comrades.

The arrival of a guest is an event. It is then that the Mongol is at his best. He is always amusing, though at times he may be a little disconcerting with his intimate questions as to one's family life and history. He wants to know all about one and has no reserve.

Wealth and status are measured by the number of sheep and horses owned. You may guess, therefore, that the horse-thief is the worst of criminals in Mongol eyes, just as he was in medieval England.

Diet consists mostly of milk, mutton, cream, and cheese made from goat's milk. Mongols are tremendous eaters, and three or four men will finish off a sheep, usually roasted whole and served sitting up on a salver. The host attacks it with a sword, handing out long strips from the back and neck and producing dainties from his own and other plates for an honoured guest.

There are no such things as regular meals, for the Mongol eats when he feels hungry. He will eat dead meat, or carrion, provided it is not too high. Half-cooked horseflesh he devours, but at a roast chicken or a boiled duck his appetite fades.

Before a meal the Mongol takes up the tea kettle and throws a drop or two in the fire. He then dips his fingers in the tea and flicks off a few more drops, this being intended to propitiate the

K 2

spirits—a vague invitation to them to join in the feast. At the end of the meal he will lick his plate as cleanly as a dog . . . and in accordance with Mongol custom I always did the same.

Women prepare the meal; they are the hewers of wood and drawers of water; they do the milking and churn the butter, and minister in every way to the wants of Mongol man.

The opium habit is not common, but everyone smokes tobacco; even the children enjoy a pipe. In China opium had such a hold that it became a real yellow peril, endangering the lives of millions. To this day, condemned prisoners in China and Mongolia are usually rendered sodden so that they will not feel the executioner's sword. As long ago as 1800 B.C. the Chinese emperor declared that opium was threatening the destruction of the Chinese people.

Opium has its devotees in the Gobi. The League of Nations found it impossible to stop the traffic, for they were up against a hidden army of agents. I was once told by an informer to go to a certain shop in a bazaar. Here I would find a mousehole— but no mice! I took the hint, searched the rooms, and sure enough found an innocent-looking hole in the boards, a closer inspection of which disclosed an opium hoard.

Mongols never walk if they can avoid it, and if a horse or camel is not available they are equally at home astride the lumbering ox.

Horse racing is popular and the Gobi produces first-rate jockeys, including women.

A Mongol race-meeting is an inspiring event. Ponies are entered by their owners and brought in from all over the country-side within a radius of two or three hundred miles. Some of these nags, although quite ready to race, have mouths of iron, and only a jockey with complete understanding of the Mongolian pony would ever get them to go between the flags. One of them I once saw was the Hyperion of the district, a whitish-black pony that won all its races in bookie-breaking fashion. The race-course boasted no tote, or Tattersall's, nor was the sunshine rent by the hoarse shouts of black forms in check trousers laying the odds. Spectators betted among themselves, odds were more often than not even, and everything was conducted in a cheerful, carefree manner.

The Newmarkets of Mongolia are not always what they seem

where racing is concerned. *Noblesse oblige* rather than superior speed often carries horses first past winning posts. The social form of owners, their wives, and influential retainers has to be studied before the form of the steeds themselves. It might be a crime in some cases for the horse of a simple herdsman to win the race when the chief's entry is competing !

§

THE EASTERN TERROR

THESE splendid riders of the plains were the originators of mounted infantry. The armies of Genghiz Khan, Kublai Khan, and Tamerlane were composed entirely of mounted men, but able to act as infantry when required. Their mobility was amazing : they would cover a thousand miles in ten days, and keep up the pace, for with plenty of led and spare horses their cruising range knew no bounds. Nations and tribes in the west, when the Mongols were on their earth-shaking expeditions, might expect them in a month or six weeks ; they would be astounded by the sudden appearance of the imperial force, for information would have told them that the enemy could not possibly be there under an estimated time. Their astonishment would very soon change to consternation. The Mongols would attack at once, like a whirlwind, with their leader always in the forefront of the battle, rallying and cheering on his troops . . . and so the day would be won . . . and the Mongols would go forward to more conquests.

The Mongol emperors maintained a regular system of relays by which they were in close touch with the capital, no matter where the army might be. These relay riders covered between them as much as four hundred miles a day. Genghiz Khan was partial to fresh fish ; and, carefully packed in ice and wet grass, it would be delivered to the royal cooks a couple of days after having been caught in the Yellow Sea, although his headquarters were nine hundred miles away.

It was their mobility which made the Mongols so formidable ; their armies were the most powerful military weapon yet forged and they were not to be beaten by serried ranks and cavalry charges. The tactics the Mongols employed were those of the Boers in South Africa. To the armies of medieval Europe the Mongols may have appeared a foe of little account, until they met them—those wild-looking riders with their high saddles, cramped seat, and rough, shaggy mounts. Yet they were all-conquering, and their ponies could live where others starved. Stout hearts, a fearless character, and the traditions of their country and leader made them enemies to be respected.

In this distant heart of Asia, at the opening of the thirteenth century, a momentous event occurred, the like of which has no parallel in history. This nomadic tribe of rough-riders of the plains, whose homes were in the Gobi, rose to fame under their leader Genghiz Khan.

Genghiz Khan with his army of horsemen swept right across Asia to Southern Germany, and when he died in 1227, he left an empire that embraced almost the whole of Asia and a large part of Europe.

The Mongol leader died, as he had lived, with his army in the field, and his last resting place is an unsolved mystery. It is known, however, this his body was brought back to the Gobi.

He introduced whirlwind methods into the art of warfare, with marching at an incredible rate, and the imposition of a will of iron upon his men. Before setting out on a campaign he devoted all his time and energy to the creation of the military machine, and while his potential enemies were oblivious of the storm that was soon to burst upon them and sat back in cushioned ease, the Mongol leader was putting in a steady twenty hours a day, working things up to a pitch of perfection and setting an almost superhuman pace.

The Mongol army was an organized fighting machine, and the wide-open spaces of the Gobi furnished the manœuvring and training ground, where drill and time schedules were carefully drawn up and divisions handled with all the zeal of a new broom.

Genghiz was a student of war ; he knew that the theatre of war is the province of strategy and that the field of battle is the province of tactics. He realized that all operations must rely for success upon power of fighting, for it is useless to conduct an army into situations which it cannot maintain in battle. He knew, too, that the object of strategy is so to direct the movements of an army that when a collision occurs it shall encounter the enemy with increased relative advantage. His methods were few and simple ; he never moved without a full knowledge of the political and military situation in the countries he was going to march against ; his intelligence service and a highly organized system of espionage kept him *au courant* with everything that was going on, while, on the other hand, his enemies were ignorant of the Mongol moves and intentions.

The advance of his Gobi riders was covered by a cloud of scouts, spread out far in advance of the divisions formed up, each in its appointed place. A drum, made from a gigantic brass basin covered with ox-hide, when beaten sounded far and wide over the plain and indicated that the army was about to march. The various divisions answered with their own drums, and then all swung into line on a front of perhaps forty or fifty miles, and, with a stentorian shout of " *hour-ra* ", moved on to battle.

Every division knew exactly what was expected of it ; the leaders worked in the closest co-operation, and kept the khan's headquarters supplied with tidings of the progress of the advance and the battle. The Mongol chief laid great stress on this matter of reports and information and the service generally was superior to anything of its kind until the coming of the railway and the telegraph.

The ways of the Mongol hosts are strangely comparable with those of the Nazis ; each moved with masses of men and employed identical tactics and terror, with mobile shock methods designed to exterminate the enemy over a wide front. The Mongols used hordes of well-trained light cavalry thoroughly conversant with their task, interspersed with armoured cavalry divisions, and the aforesaid screen of scouts covering the operations, denying all information to the enemy and keeping him in constant doubt about the Mongol intentions. A Mongol descent was strikingly similar to the sudden appearance of the Nazi hosts from the forests of the Ardennes in the invasion of France of 1940—no one expected it, nor was there any reliable information about the modern Mongol move.

In the above formation they came on, spreading like locusts and leaving behind the pyramids of skulls. The gas chambers of the Nazi can be likened to these pyramids.

These forerunners of the Nazis were the high wind that swept out of Asia, the winged killers who knew not fear or mercy ; they were the panzers of their day, moving without need of petrol. How they rode ! A Mongol army could vie with the swiftest tanks ; the speed of their coming almost amounted to witchcraft and confounded all notions of warfare, causing the ordinary canons of generalship and defence of those times to be hopelessly out of date.

Time and again the enemy loitered along lines of deceptive security, awaiting the Mongol onslaught with well-fortified confidence . . . and then the situation changed with a terrible swiftness that nullified all resistance. The Mongol magic, supported by the best reconnaissance organization ever evolved, worked to its predestined end . . . the spell of speed succeeded.

With the rising of the sun the horizon was bare and empty of menace, all seemed well, with no enemy in sight and nothing to warrant any suspicion of impending danger. They had been lulled into a sense of false security ; why should not life go on like this . . . in calm beatitude ? Then hardly before the sun had climbed into the sky the rush appeared . . . over the horizon came the Eastern terror with hurricane intensity, bearing down with a force that nothing on earth could stop. The wondering and bewildered enemy rubbed their eyes in astonishment and saw a vast host riding out of the east, riding like men possessed, riding as men had never ridden before.

Here were the Mongol horned standards, carried aloft and streaming in the wind, the horses going all-out like the Scots Greys at Waterloo, the ground shaking with the thunder of their hoofs, and the air rent with the " *hour-ras* " given by myriads of men . . . here were the redoubtable roundheads of Asia charging into battle. And as they came within bow-shot clouds of arrows darkened the sky, striking down the foe from afar.

What a scene ! One moment the horizon held life and light, the next it had become grim and dark, with the arrival of death on horseback. Neither to right nor left was there any way of escape for the bemused forces facing this mounted Nemesis ; all

A giant prayer-wheel of lacquered yak-hide.

The abbot of a monastery turns his hand prayer-wheel.

Though they wash only twice in a lifetime, these Tibetans seem happy enough.

A lama ceremonial orchestra is a picturesque affair, with the musicians' costumes differing according to the kind of instruments they play. The big horns, those in the lower picture, are often over eight feet in length, and emit an eerie, deep, booming note which echoes among the mountains and valleys of this part of the Gobi Desert.

lines of retreat were closed by charging mounted warriors, and when they turned round to seek safety in headlong flight they found this last line of hope denied to them by an encircling band of Mongols directed with all the well-mapped precision of masters of the art of war.

Now, what caused the decline of the Mongols ?

There are a number of causes, perhaps not the least being religion. This was Lamaism, a perverted form of Buddhism. It was Kublai Khan who directed that this ritualistic form of Buddhism should become the Mongol faith, and it was he who ordered the destruction of the religious literature of other creeds. With the coming of Lamaism the warlike qualities of the Mongols deteriorated, for it is a pacifist creed, and we have seen what a large proportion of Mongol manhood is to be found in monasteries, following the lazy life of the lama.

The conquests of Genghiz Khan and successive leaders could not last for long with the domestic warfare springing up in the Mongol ranks and the lapse to Lamaism. The links in the chain of empire were snapping ; internal trouble, too much luxury, the fading glamour of conquest, a faith that stultified effort and ambition ; all these things brought about a gradual decay.

The Mongols were a horde of warriors who loved war for its own sake ; they brought no culture into conquered lands, and so nothing remains as a monument to creative genius. They were in many ways the greatest warriors in history, and when under such leaders as Genghiz Khan and Tamerlane, nothing could withstand them.

Only one obstacle could stop these riders of the Gobi—the sea. They knew all about the movement and supply of armies on land, but few, if any, of the Mongols had ever seen the sea or a ship, and the transport of troops across the ocean and their supply from a sea base was a branch of the military art beyond their ken.

STRANGE CUSTOMS

MONGOLIA is still a home of sorcery and magic such as existed in Europe in the Middle Ages. In the mountains, along the southern and western borders of the Gobi, are hermits and holy men gazing down in silent contemplation on the earth below and around them. By concentration of mind and contemplative powers, they have attained a seemingly magical strength. I have heard of lamas or priests who wander from camp to camp and, gaining control of their breathing, are able to raise themselves in the air off the ground, hear with their diaphragms, and breathe through their ears. Some, by employing their spirit bodies, claim ability to fly through the air with the wind, transport themselves to the tops of mountains, and pass through keyholes—to make use, in fact, of powers supposed to belong to fairy tales.

They first gain control of the conscious body. Once this is dominated, they advance to other spheres, using their spirit bodies.

While travelling across high plateaux, I once came across some executioners endeavouring to drown a lama of unusual power, for some political crime he had committed. This lama had a large stone tied round his neck and other stones were attached to his legs. He had been thrown into a turbulent river and left there for several minutes, until it seemed certain he must be drowned and dead. Yet when he was pulled out he was very much alive. With shouts and yells his executioners hurled him back once more into the river from which he had so miraculously escaped. Once again he sank beneath the water, weighted down as he was with the heavy stones. The men kept pulling at the ropes which were attached to him, just as though they were fishermen expecting a good bite at the end of their lines. They left him there for at least double the time sufficient to drown any ordinary man; then they pulled the body out, and the old lama was still alive.

The gaolers themselves were astounded; some of them went

down on their knees imploring pardon of the man they supposed to be too holy to die. They could not understand such a phenomenon.

One of the things these tribes of the Gobi did not like was whistling—whereby hangs a tale. In the valleys and ravines that lead over the Roof of the World, the men who carry your kit will tell you on no account to whistle. Not only will it bring down avalanches and snowslides, but will arouse the anger of the gods.

Once during a halt at a Mongol camp I whistled. The Mongol chief was alarmed. Disaster, he said, would descend upon the camp, and what was I going to do about it ? I did not want to upset these people, for they were very helpful and I had to depend upon them for the rest of my journey through that largely unexplored land.

I had to think quickly.

I knew the Mongol penchant for strong drink, and realizing that this would be the key to reopen the door to peace and friendship, I produced a bottle of cherry brandy. The effect was magical ; I handed it to my host, he ran his fingers over the label and smelt the contents. His demeanour changed entirely, he bowed low . . . and thereafter got dreadfully drunk, and when I left the next morning insisted on my being made a life member of the tribe ; so I felt that whistling has its compensations !

As I have said, the Mongols are a nation of riders and shepherds ; but among the lamas, or priests, who constitute one-fifth of the population, the medical profession is popular, since it affords an opportunity of acquiring wealth and status among the people. Doctors, as a rule, are paid when patients are well ; salaries are stopped when a person becomes ill, and doctors are summoned to live in a patient's house till he either gets better or dies. Their knowledge of medicine is founded on superstition and witchcraft, by means of which diseases are treated, drugs and medicines receiving only secondary consideration. It is a curious fact, however, that the Mongol does to some extent believe in medicine, and the more objectionable and nauseous it is the more readily he will swallow it.

Once the person falls ill the medico takes up residence and remains there, doing himself well and partaking of the best.

The payment-by-results method is one that might with advantage be sometimes adopted in the West !

In keeping with the basic principles of their religion, the Mongols have queer ideas touching the origin of complaints from which they may be suffering. A Mongol once declared to me, with all sincerity, that the deity was angry with him and had visited him with a fever because he had inadvertently cut a stick from the stunted trees surrounding a desert monastery. Another, who had the world's worst cold, put it down to the anger of the gods at his having destroyed life in the shape of worms and insects when moving camp.

Whilst on the subject of medicos and medicine, one of the cardinal rules, I was told, is never to allow the patient to sleep in the daytime. Further, the Mongol lama has the idea that there are three pulses in each human wrist, one side being yellow blood from the bile and liver, one quite colourless, and the third red from the heart.

Like the Chinese, Mongol practitioners are curious examples of the surgeon and the doctor in this land of wonder and mystery. They assert that the body is divided into squares, each one of which has direct relation with some particular organ. There are, they say, three hundred and sixty-seven such squares, and each disease or complaint must be treated through the square to which it refers. If it is in the waist, the small of the back, or the stomach, the square of that part must be pierced by a needle, usually red-hot, and so the doctor goes on puncturing his patients until they either recover or succumb to the ordeal by fire.

I once had a servant who suffered from fever ; he consulted his medical attendant, who promptly punctured him in the neck and down the back. Either the shock of the red-hot needles drove the fever out, or my man decided it was better to get well on his own, while the prospects were bright ; for the doctor, in search of a cure, was determined to go on puncturing in front as well as behind.

The professional story-teller is another feature of Mongolian life, as he is, indeed, throughout China. This teller of tales has a unique place among the people and the monasteries. His stories of the long-ago stir their imaginations, and make even the common people and the monks conversant with the early history of their territory. It is their form of history, and the story-teller omits little in his telling, the most minute details being given. The crowd squat round a visiting story-teller, and their faces light up with pleasure at the mention of certain famous and heroic names. They are never weary of hearing how the heroes of the past won renown.

The best story-tellers are usually those from the more intellectual of the monastic order. Their stories are always far-fetched and they trade upon the credulity of the people ; indeed, it is largely why they maintain a hold on the country. The story-tellers and the monasteries go hand in hand, and so we will turn to them and the controlling heads of this vast religious organization.

§

THE HIGH PRIESTS OF BUDDHISM

MONASTERIES, dark and cold, are strange storehouses of make-believe in Mongolia. Here are the doctors, priests, bankers, and governors.

I found lamas dedicated to eternal solitude, to the study of ancient mysteries, or the worship of the higher peaks. South of the Gobi, in the Karakoram Mountains, live monks who continually pray for the sins of the world. Day and night mean nothing to them. Their vows prevent them from talking, walking, or having intimacy with any living soul. Buried alive in bee-hive cells at the foot of the mother monastery, they vow themselves to years of silence and imprisonment. Their food is bread and water, and they concentrate on the spirit world until they see visions and become mere ghosts of ordinary men.

There are two principal living deities in Mongol Buddhism ; the Dalai Lama, who lives at Lhasa, the capital of Tibet, and the Hu-tuk-tu, residing at Urga, or Ulan Bator Hoto, in the eastern Gobi. Both are held in the highest veneration by the Mongols, and Urga is regarded by them as the second sacred city of the world, the first being Lhasa.

There is also the Tashi Lama, who is the second in the lama hierarchy ; but he is more strictly concerned with Tibet, where he lives at Tashilumpo, this having been his official residence since 1663.

As the Dalai Lama is the most important person in our survey, I will give an account of him ; the more so as I myself came into contact with this Pope of Buddhism.

The Dalai Lama, Vice-Regent of the Buddha on earth, the Sea of Wisdom, the Ocean of Merit, the All-Knowing Presence, and All-seeing Eye, is supreme, and is a non-stop ruler who never dies, for it is said that his spirit passes into that of his successor the moment he leaves this earth. He is the head of all the Buddhist priesthood, a pontiff wielding immense spiritual and temporal power. His rule dates from the eighth century, and his palace in Lhasa is an imposing building with hundreds of rooms and halls. So holy was Lhasa that in a hundred years only three European explorers were able to set foot in the Forbidden City. Until the British expedition of 1904 the Tibetan frontier was closed to foreigners, and even now it is not easy to gain admittance.

When organizing the expedition that flew over Mount Everest a few years ago, I found that, according to Lamaist doctrines, it was to the Dalai Lama, as supreme ruler of the country, we should apply for permission to pass over the mountain, the home of the gods. The truth is that on hearing that two " giant birds " were to fly over Mount Everest, the Dalai Lama wrote to the Government of India saying that he and his people viewed the idea with great disquietude . . . and what were we going to do about it ? The communication was handed to me, and I replied that nothing was further from our thoughts than to disturb the heavenly bodies, and that the gods might rest happy and undisturbed . . . which they did.

We had to remember that, to the inhabitants of Mongolia and Tibet, the high mountains are the abodes of gods and goddesses ; every one of the higher peaks of a mountain range is the home of a spirit, either good or evil, and over all looms the figure and personality of the Dalai Lama.

As we have seen, the Dalai Lama is supposed never to die ; he indicates who will be his reincarnated self and that person

becomes his successor. If this is not done the succession is in
the hands of a selected band of lamas who go out into the high-
ways and byways, with oracular and astrological revelations, and
search for the child. This is what happened when the late
Dalai Lama died a few years ago. All Mongolia and Tibet were
anxiously waiting for the new priest, but two years passed before
the discovery of the infant who was destined to become a
god.

This child ruler, when discovered, becomes the all-powerful
leader of millions of people, both in spiritual and temporal
affairs ; he is High Priest as well as King. Every woman in
the country hopes she may be the proud mother of the new
Dalai Lama. No film star will ever get more publicity than this
child, and no national sweepstake could be more exciting in its
results.

According to general belief, each succeeding Dalai Lama is
the reincarnation of the former holder of the office, and is born
as nearly as possible at the time when his predecessor died. The
lucky family who can claim the new birth are forthwith ennobled.
Estates are granted to them and titles bestowed, so that there is
never any lack of candidates for this unique competition.

Before the old Dalai Lama dies he usually tells where and how
he will reincarnate and come back to the world, giving, in some
cases, details which help to identify his successor. The search
does not begin until a year after his death.

Various mystic signs and symbols are associated with the
appearance of the newcomer. The child usually has long lobes
to his ears, highly-arched eyebrows, and though less than two
years old, can sometimes talk quite easily. Generally he is the
possessor of a beautiful smile. A close scrutiny is also made of
the sunburns placed at birth upon the shoulders of all infants, a
disc of metal, representing the configuration of the moon,
augmenting these birth marks with its distinct point. The
child, therefore, must have his moon mark corresponding almost
exactly with the date of death of the previous Dalai Lama to be
considered for the post of successor.

If there are a number of candidates, resort is made to a weeding-
out process, the names being written on pieces of gold paper,
carried to Lhasa and placed in a golden urn from which they are

drawn out—choosing a ruler according to the will of destiny, or in accordance with chance.

The Dalai Lama occupies an extraordinary position among present-day dictators of mankind. None may look at him until leave is granted; all must bow and remain with faces to the ground. He may not marry, nor touch alcohol, and if he eats meat religious ceremonies have to be performed at each meal to ensure that the animal will live again in a higher state of existence.

What a strange picture he represents! What an unequal drama of motherhood and birth! In no other time or place has there been a babe so extolled, venerated, and worshipped by millions of people as this non-stop ruler. He sits on a cushion with a silver tassel in his hand, and only on rare occasions is he allowed to see women. Thousands of pilgrims flock to get a glimpse of the holiest living symbol of Buddhism, often travelling great distances to obtain his blessing.

Only one woman is ever seen on equal terms by the Dalai Lama; a reincarnation belonging to a different monastery. It is believed she can turn people into pigs if she feels strong displeasure, and for this reason she is called " The Thunderbolt Sow ".

Although the prestige of the two heads of Buddhism, the one in Tibet and the other in the Gobi, is great, and although they are still surrounded by age-old ritual, modernization is creeping in. The prayer-wheels, once hand- or water-driven, are now said to be imported often from abroad and worked by electric batteries. Then, a year or two ago, the Dalai Lama bought a baby car which we sent to him from India. The electric light has come into its own at Lhasa, and you can talk on the telephone from India to the Tibetan capital.

Urga is the largest town in the Gobi desert, its importance being derived from the fact that it was the home of the Living Buddha—the Hu-tuk-tu, to whom the Mongols made pilgrimages in order to have the privilege of gazing upon the features of their living god. Since the coming of the so-called republic the Hu-tuk-tu has fallen from his high estate and is no longer the personality of old.

The Hu-tuk-tu led a life of the strictest privacy in an imposing

A devil-dancer—he frightens away the
demons by the god's armchair !

The Potala—the palace of the ruler and
High Priest of Tibet, the Dalai Lama.

palace like the potala at Lhasa. It is a building of Tibetan and Mongolian architecture, painted white, red and gold, and is crowned by a cupola which has a curious resemblance to an ornament on top of a huge wedding cake.

Like his superior, the Dalai Lama, his prestige was due to the fact that he was held to be a man who had won the right to Nirvana, but had consented to rebirth for the sake of his fellow-men, and as he had, amongst other things, control over the evil spirits, he was revered by the people.

The Mongols had an exaggerated idea of the power and scope of the Hu-tuk-tu ; they associated him with occult and other arts, and still say that lamas of his standing can achieve anything by a life of continual prayer and self-denial. From time immemorial there have been those among them who have given up their lives to the study of the imperfections of our human frame. Various wonders in the medical and other worlds of science have, so it is declared, come down to them from years that date from before the advent of the Buddha.

Day and night, generation after generation, lamas of the higher orders have been studying and adding to the store of knowledge which their forefathers possessed. It is even said that they hold the secret of life and death—some of their experiments in surgery are certainly startling. To what extent this is true none can tell, for, as yet, no one has ever succeeded in getting behind the scenes in the lama world, and so we have to rely mainly on conjecture.

There is a curious and sinister side to the life of the Dalai Lama and his *confrère* the Hu-tuk-tu. They seldom live beyond the age of twenty or so ; the late Dalai Lama was a record in this respect, for he survived to the age of sixty, all his four predecessors having died before they were nineteen, just as they came into power. Until attaining that age they are subject to a regent, and to the strong and ambitious ones it is not desirable for the high-priest to take over charge ! The late Dalai Lama, however, outwitted all attempts to make an end of him and reigned undisturbed for forty-one years.

The palace of the Hu-tuk-tu at Urga had many priceless relics ; tiny chapels with old images, some of which came from distant parts of India and China ; pieces of porcelain that would command a fortune in a London saleroom, cloisonné jars and bowls, worn with age but of wonderful beauty.

A highlight of this quaint palace was the silence that prevailed both inside and out. Although there are forty-five thousand people living in the town, with herds of cattle, horses, and camels, the only sound that disturbed the almost uncanny stillness was the clang of brass and copper bells from the temples when a festival or other ceremony was in vogue, and the grinding motion and creak of the prayer-wheels as they were turned by the faithful. The tea-caravans that come up from China and the Great Wall swung silently to one side of the great palace in order not to disturb the peace and serenity of the living Buddha.

After the palace, the lamaserai, or temple, was the principal structure in Urga ; it was a wooden building without windows and lighted by oil wicks in big bowls that sent up streams of black and sooty smoke, so that it was extremely difficult to obtain a view of the statue of the Buddha, said to be the largest in the world, standing over a hundred feet in height, and made entirely of gilt bronze. How they managed to get the statue into position, let alone to forge and bring it there, is beyond comprehension. At the foot of the statue, which was in perfect proportion, were a number of small figures of Mongol horsemen, looking lifelike, with painted hands and faces. There are also many large and beautifully worked silk prayer-flags, dating back several centuries, old and worn like the battle-standards at Versailles.

The general gloom and absence of windows prevented a real appreciation of this temple ; it was all very old and inspiring, until one noticed the throne of the Hu-tuk-tu on one side of the statue . . . a cheap and rickety chair of gold and tinsel, the sort of thing one might expect to see in a country fair or a circus. It was the one discordant note.

Out in the desert beyond the palace and the town is the burial ground. The Mongols retain customs and beliefs the origin of which must be sought far back in the mists of antiquity. The disposal of the dead is a striking example of this. Instead of burial in the usual manner the body is put out on a knoll, or some slight rising ground, and there left to the mercy of dogs and birds of prey, which has given rise to the Chinese saying that the raven is the Mongol's coffin. Consequently the ground is covered with skulls and bones, and dogs and birds carry on a constant fight for the bits and pieces.

Some of the Mongol clans take this a stage further in the way of the weird and the unusual. Should the remains not be disposed of within a few days the deceased is considered to have led a wicked and wayward life, since even the dogs and birds are shocked and refuse to touch the body. The sequel to this discovery is the rounding up of the members of the deceased's family, who are all given a sound beating with the idea of saving them from the fate of the dead relative.

In the eastern Gobi the corpse is sometimes placed on a cart and driven at full speed across the plain, the jolting dislodging it from the vehicle; but the driver dashes on with redoubled energy, never daring to look back, for to do so would bring the evil spirits upon him, and only when he is certain the body is no longer on the cart does he rein in and offer a prayer to the gods.

Urga is largely a town of felt tents, for the Mongol never lives in a house if he can avoid it. One or two of the permanent buildings are of brick and stone and wood; and there is usually a police station, or guard house, where offenders are dealt with.

The prison system and mode of punishment are dark and grim; they take one back to the Middle Ages of Europe, to the dungeons of the Inquisition, and all the horrors of those times, when much ingenuity was displayed in the invention of punishments.

Here in the Gobi offenders are treated in a ghastly and original manner. A man may have been convicted of horse-thieving, or some similar offence, which is a particular outrage of Mongol codes of honour. Genghiz Khan had his own way of dealing with such criminals; he would tie heavy bags of sand round their necks and make them walk all day without a rest, thirty and forty miles . . . and if they fell by the wayside, they were helped on to the next world.

In more modern days they put the man in an oblong box, about five feet by two, and two feet in depth; it is the counterpart of a coffin, and there, chained and manacled, he is left to pass weeks, sometimes months, and not infrequently a year—it all depends upon the nature of the crime. The wretched man can neither stand up nor lie down, but must perforce assume a semi-crouching posture, with the result that the limbs become shrunken and useless, and after a time he is nothing but a shrivelled wreck from the constant agonizing position to which he is subjected. He is taken out for a few minutes daily, food is passed to him through a small hole in the side of the box, and for covering at night he has a thin worn blanket, this being exchanged in the winter for a sheepskin coat, both coverings totally inadequate as bedclothes, especially when the thermometer drops to twenty degrees below zero. Indeed, how a prisoner could survive the torture of this coffin, the disgusting food, and the unspeakable filth, was always beyond me.

§

THE LAMAS

THE lamas are the real governors in the Gobi and Mongolia. Generally speaking they are a nondescript crowd, living on the credulity of the people, and I doubt if for incompetence, sloth, and crime their equals could be found.

The monasteries are the preaching and ruling institutions. They also take the place of inns and at most of them the traveller can find food and shelter. The fare is simple, but good ; it is the highest comfort the country can offer, though pots and pans may be dirty and the hands of the host grimy from neglect of soap and water.

All over the high territory of Central Asia and Mongolia there is the same belief in gods and demi-gods who inhabit the mountain peaks. Devils are supposed to come up from under the ground, and Mongols are always erecting shrines to keep the devils in their proper place. I came upon many conducted parties going with their prayer-wheels and banners to pay calls on mountains. A lama told me that anyone who dies on the slopes of a lofty mountain is thought to have incurred the wrath of the gods.

There is a holy place in Mongolia, a kind of Glastonbury of the snows, to enter which monks have to pass high novitiate and become holy men. Lamas here rise at three a.m. and go to bed with the sun. Time is nothing to them, and they concern themselves only with the millions who are loaded with sin, and the millions yet unborn who may be turned into the right path by prayer.

In these monasteries the maze of alleyways and draughty cells, the eerie light, the welcoming ceremonies, the rancid-buttered tea, the silver cups, the jewels mined from the hills, and the long Chinese carpets all provide spectacle and contrast.

When you enter, the monks line up on the roof with their band; the trumpets, ten feet long or more, are supported by small boys. You are given tea, flavoured with that rancid butter, and a cold hard granite cell for a bedroom, with no bed of down or feathers, but a mattress of rock. A brazier stuck in a crevice in the wall may afford warmth. The soup for your dinner looks like dish-water. In this fluid float a few morsels of meat. You drink it as you would a glass of water, or use a travelling cup, which I always carried.

When you retire you see monks robed like those of the Inquisition flitting about during every hour of darkness. They are keeping watch . . . but they tend to turn pleasant dreams into nightmares.

If you have an audience with the head of a monastery there is little or no conversation. Sufficient merit lies in mere contact with the divine. I heard of one audience with a grand lama who was silent all the time; but so powerful was his personality that all there were of the opinion that they were looking at one of the finest actors—or else one of the holiest men—they had ever met.

Lamas number about one-fifth of the population. Though not intellectuals, they possess a strong spiritual sense. A lama hopes to lose himself in the hereafter.

There are pilgrims who visit monasteries in the Gobi, Urga, the Rome of the country, or Lhasa, the capital of the Dalai Lama, and measure the whole distance by throwing themselves full-length on the ground. Then they get up, and where their hands have touched the ground, they repeat the process, and so on to their destination. They may take a year or more to accomplish their task. I once met a pilgrim who had been thirteen months at it. He was held in great esteem afterwards.

The monks in mountain and desert salute the spirits on long trombones. They play shrieking notes that are curiously like cat-calls, while long, weird calls shock the silence and echo down the valleys. This wild music that takes the place of an organ, though decidedly original, would soon empty a western church.

These monasteries, utterly lonely and remote, lie in a fantastic setting of pinnacles and icicles that form part of glaciers extending for long distances. In the moonlight they glint, in the sunshine they shimmer; they are the lamps of the gods and demi-gods who, the people believe, hold suzerainty over the high places.

Mountains give out a spell, they say. Lamas and monks gaze at these white-topped peaks; people bring offerings of tea, milk, honey, and barley. They set up prayer-wheels, and light fires of juniper.

The heart of Asia still holds first place in the realm of mystery and romance, especially that unexplored corner of the Kuen Lun Mountains in south-eastern Turkistan, where the Chinese hold shadowy dominion over the highest inhabited portion of the globe, a mountain maze that looks out on to the Gobi and is still a sealed book to the rest of the world.

There I found a strange Buddhist sect who have as near neighbours more than a score of peaks exceeding a height of twenty-three thousand feet, and glaciers covering hundreds of square miles.

This curious sect, numbering not more than six hundred, are doing penance for the rest of the world, for the sins of you and me and all mankind, and in their monastery hewn out of the solid rock they are completely isolated from the world beyond, unmindful of wars and upheavals and the rise and fall of empires. They are following what they conceive to be the original precepts of their ancient religion, as expounded by the Buddha six hundred years before the birth of Christ.

I will pass over the journey thither and come direct to the discovery of the monastery.

I and my small party had reached it after infinite toil and pain amidst the rapids and ravines of the world's highest range.

For days we had run the gauntlet of snow-slides and avalanches, and at dusk reached the summit of a pass—at an altitude of eighteen thousand feet—beyond which lay the monastery I was in search of.

Slowly we worked our way to the foot of the pass, over glaciers and along the edge of yawning crevasses, by walls of snow and ice, and across torrents that swept through the canyon like a mill-race, where one false step when jumping from rock to rock meant an icy grave.

Picture to yourself the canyon, which varied from thirty to seventy yards broad, its sides towering sheer for at least six thousand feet, and above them glaciers and peaks until the wall was more than two miles in height.

At dusk we reached a point where the canyon widened to some two hundred yards, with a patch of barley, the only cereal growing at this altitude, whence a rocky path led off into a side ravine to the monastery. The noise of the water was deafening, and the track so steep and narrow that in places two people could not possibly have passed each other, while frequently it ran flush with the cliff-side, with a drop of more than a thousand feet into the torrent below.

Finally we reached a clearing at a sudden turn in the path and saw before us a rough stone structure built into and alongside the edge of the ravine. Remembering its reputation, its inaccessibility, and the weird stories connected with the sect, I could not help wondering what would happen once inside the monastery.

I had intended camping without, but the abbot, who greeted me dressed in a dirty yellow robe and with a shaven pate, insisted on my staying within the great building, so, accepting his hospitality, I followed him through the gateway.

Here other monks joined us, dressed in long coarse robes, similar to those of monks in Europe, and together we passed up a flight of stone steps into a corridor that seemed to be hollowed out of the mountain. We went along this passage for perhaps seventy yards, then branched off into a smaller one that twisted and turned until I lost all sense of direction.

At last we reached a small door on which the abbot knocked. It was swung back and we filed through. All this time not a sound had been uttered, the whole place was wrapped in semi-darkness, and the air of mystery and the general uncanny procedure of my ghostly attendants was far from cheering.

We next ascended a spiral stairway which led to a small landing lighted by a long slit in the wall, from which I gathered that we must be at the side of the monastery overlooking the ravine ; but the crevice in the wall being ten feet above me I was uncertain of my bearings.

From the landing we entered a room like a cell, about ten feet by six feet, and at least twenty feet in height. In one corner was a narrow ledge of rock that served as a bed, a rough chair of wood and goatskin, and a large earthern pitcher. This was all it contained, and as the other rooms leading off from it and the landing were bare of any furniture, I had perforce to consider myself domiciled in luxury.

The etiquette of the monastery apparently required that all conversation should be in so low a tone as to be practically whispered.

The abbot served tea flavoured with rancid butter, and some coarse brown cakes resembling oaten cakes, but nothing like so palatable as the Highland variety. However, I was both hungry and thirsty, so the frugal repast was as corn in Egypt.

Having started me on the meal, the abbot departed with his attendant monks, adding that so long as I was within the monastic walls he considered me as his guest, and all my wants would be ministered to by himself or his immediate entourage.

Now, although I have a fair bump of locality, I realized how difficult it would be to find my way out into the open should necessity arise ; but dismissing such possibilities from my mind, I sat down on the ledge and awaited developments.

Night closed over the lonely monastery, and after another scanty meal I wrapped myself in my blankets and lay down on my rocky couch. The wind moaned and shrieked through the crevice and up the stairway, the light from an oil lamp on the floor throwing weird shadows across the room, while anon, dark figures, silent and ghostly, passed in front of the door. Once or twice during the night I awoke from a fitful sleep and found a cloaked and spectral figure making a tour of my room.

At last, some time before dawn, I heard the low chant of

voices in unison, a wailing note as of souls in torment. I jumped up and went to the doorway : not a sign of anyone, only the distant sound of that depressing dirge.

Perhaps it was a midnight service ? As I stood there listening a shadow appeared upon the wall and a huge bat flashed past within an inch of my face. It galvanized me into activity, and, donning coat and boots, I set off down the passage in the direction of the music.

Threading many passages, twisting and turning this way and that, I came to an open doorway with a veranda beyond it, then a courtyard leading to a building opposite. I crossed the courtyard and peered in through the half-closed doorway.

Before me was a chamber about one hundred and twenty feet long and sixty or seventy broad. It was but dimly lighted, with oil and wicks in clay bowls, emitting volumes of black soot and smoke. Kneeling on the stone floor were the members of this extraordinary sect, droning the songs of remorse, bewailing the sins of those countless millions who had gone before, of those millions scattered over the earth's wide surface who were still a living force, and of those millions yet unborn whom it might be possible to turn into the right path.

Picture, if you can, that courtyard set in an amphitheatre of mountains, the loftiest peaks in the world, the pale light of the moon, the ghostly oil lamps, and the hundreds of kneeling figures intoning that supreme chant to an omnipotent power. It would have stirred the feelings of a Nero.

As I retraced my steps across the courtyard I heard faint sounds of voices from the side flush with the mountain. Curiosity, or perhaps irresistible fascination, drew me there. I saw openings some eighteen inches square in the rock, and from them there issued a similar chant as that from the great hall.

Was it an echo or merely an hallucination ? I struck a match and peered through one of the openings. Gradually the form of a human being with emaciated figure and glassy eyes became visible in the light. It seemed to be looking at me from another world. Then it lowered its eyes and continued the chant.

I hurried from the courtyard, from those living tombs, regained my room, and lay down, but not to sleep. Dawn came, and with it my departure from the monastery towards that great world of sin and sorrow, with its wars and upheavals and all the consequences that come in their wake.

§

THE KHAN OF THE KALMUCKS

To the south-west of the Gobi, and forming its border line there, is the Great Yulduz Valley, the home of the direct descendants of the Mongol horde, the Kalmucks; who, although they have now come under Chinese influence, have preserved their own language, as well as national customs and traditions, many of which are remarkably interesting.

The Kalmucks were great fighters and travellers, and adventure is the highlight of their history. After many wanderings hither and thither, they were settled during the eighteenth century on the Volga under Russian jurisdiction; but, becoming dissatisfied with life there, and the Russians'—perhaps with memories of the days of Genghiz Khan and Tamerlane—not treating them too well, they determined on a flight eastwards across the Asiatic steppes, to some land where they might find a haven of refuge.

So, in 1771, took place the migration of the Kalmucks to that remote corner of the old Mongol empire, a trek immortalized by De Quincey in his *Flight of a Tartar Tribe*. This celebrated journey, surpassing that of the Boer trek from Cape Colony in 1836 to what is now the Transvaal, occupied eight months, and although at the outset they were half-a-million strong, only one-fifth survived to reach the goal. For months they struggled on, battling with a constancy that has no parallel in history against Russian, Kirghiz, and Cossack, with the horrors of the Central Asiatic winter, hunger, fatigue, and disease. Through it all they fought on, paying no heed where they went and caring for nothing but to put as great a distance as possible between themselves and their pursuers. At last, when they felt they could go no farther, they reached their goal, unmindful of the fact that they had achieved one of the greatest exploits of all time.

The Chinese took them in, " shooed " off their pursuers, and so the Kalmucks settled down in this new home, where there was ample pasturage for their herds of cattle and horses.

Like their brothers to the north, east, and west, the Kalmucks are Buddhists. They wear their hair in short pigtails, a survival of the old days. They are great hunters, and I spent three happy months with them hunting the Asiatic wapiti stag, ibex, and other game in the forests and on the rocky heights.

The mode of life, manners, and customs of the Kalmucks are similar to those of the rest of the Mongol race, and they have many strange beliefs. They tell you that the fox is of a black colour for five hundred years, after which he changes to white for a similar period. At the end of a thousand years, having wearied of life and whiteness, he gladly dies.

Of pine and fir trees, the Kalmucks say that they stand for a thousand years ; then fall to the ground and lie another thousand years until they rot, and that the wood from those trees is the best for camp fires and calls up the good spirits of the past.

They are a jovial people and love a wedding, which is at once a glamorous ceremony, a cross-country race, and a tournament, for the bride has to fight possibly half-a-dozen bridegrooms. This is what happens.

The bride is wooed and won on horseback, and she leads off at full gallop, arrayed in her best finery. At other times she is a sooty Cinderella, but on her wedding day she appears like a dainty princess, with a long coloured coat fastened by a sash at the waist, and a hat shaped like an inverted saucer, with stand-up edges decked out in vari-coloured tassels. Top-boots and a riding-whip complete her equipment, and she is ready for the meet.

If she is the belle of the camp there is always a number of suitors. The lady has to be captured in a game which might well be termed a love chase. This is the big moment of her life as, Daphne-like, she flies in this race from the Apollos, among whom there is always one she is keen on—and that one she is going to accept. So she takes the lead in a breakneck race against all the lads who aspire to her hand.

To level matters up and give the bride a fair chance, she carries a raw-hide whip with which she can, and does, slash away

the attention of undesirables.   It is a joy to watch the horsemanship and thrills of such a game ; a sight that Olympia would be
delighted to acclaim.

One of these girls was a daughter of the morning, and she rode
like a winged being.   The wings of love and her superb horsemanship lent her a sort of distinction, so that she was as one
inspired.   Each time an undesirable came too close the stinging
lash of her whip told him clearly to keep off.   And when
the right man caught up and the whip was no longer hers to
wield, she led him such a chase, and eluded him so often, that
one wondered how the thing was possible without many active
rehearsals.   Here were these nomadic people displaying feats of
horsemanship that few trick riders in Europe or America could
emulate.

Here, in the Yulduz Valley, lives also the Khan of the Kalmucks,
who claims descent from Genghiz Khan.   He is the liege lord
of all his nomad subjects and rather like a character out of a novel.
Before I came to the Kalmuck country I had heard much about
the Khan and his people, and so determined to pay him a visit.
Long weeks of hard marching brought me there, over high
mountains and through deep valleys, across the Roof of the
World, journeying onward, ever onward, into this land of old
Tartary.   It may be a long, long way to Tipperary, but it struck
me as being no mean distance to the land of the Kalmucks.

At last I came to the eastern end of the Yulduz Valley, and
camped one night by a group of auls where I had a talk with an
intelligent Kalmuck.   He told me their Khan " lived a great way
off ", but his idea as to the exact distance was vague.   However,
he volunteered to go with me, and so I and my party started at
dawn the next morning.

Fresh horses had been secured and we made our way along
the valley, following a track through picturesque scenery.   With
the exception of a few other Kalmucks and a camel team laden
with tea going down, like the caravans in the Bible, to barter
amongst the tribes, we met few people.   At dusk, after
fourteen hours in the saddle, we came to a Kalmuck camp by the
bank of a river, where fresh horses were again provided.   As we
rode off the sun was declining behind the mountains to the
westward, long shadows fell across the valley, and the evening

wind sprang up and moaned among the rocks as we plunged into the river.

Three times we had to ford that river, which was wide and deep, and only by the greatest exertions could our horses hold their own ; the water was as cold as ice and the current ran like a mill-race, while the depth in places might have been up to fifty or sixty feet, though I could only judge it by the shelving of the banks. For some distance, in black darkness for the last two crossings, the Kalmuck and I battled on side by side, with the whole force of the river against us ; but we managed it in the end.

Beyond the third ford we met some more travellers who told us the Khan's camp was still " a long way off " and that there were at least five hundred auls there. It was ten o'clock when we stumbled on a tiny camp, and here my guide wanted to stay the night, but I persuaded him to go on. I was weary myself of the long ride, for we had now been eighteen hours on the move and the apparently phantom home of the Khan seemed farther off than ever.

At last, when already one o'clock in the morning, we came out of a narrow opening in the hills on to a wide and level valley, and in another half-mile gained the outer ring of the Khan's camp.

In the moonlight I could see the valley filled with auls. " The home of the Khan," said the Kalmuck guide, as we halted to survey the scene.

I looked across the valley, hardly able to believe that we had, at last, arrived at the camp of which I had heard so much. There stood the auls, dark and ghostly. We began moving towards them and must have been a quarter of a mile away when a new sound broke upon our ears—the barking of dogs. Soon we were to see what gigantic dogs they were. It was now two o'clock in the morning ; we had been nineteen hours in the saddle ; but we were there.

I had a feeling of strange excitement and expectancy, almost as if I had stepped back into the Middle Ages and was journeying with Marco Polo. We pushed on at a steady trot, when suddenly we were surrounded by fifty or sixty dogs who gave us the most boisterous welcome. The din they created was terrific ; they were real disturbers of the peace in that quiet valley of the Heavenly Mountains, and, as guardians of the camp, they were determined to justify the trust. Nothing we could do served to quell the interrupters of the night's serenity; the Kalmuck guide did his best, but he might as well have tried to cleave the pillar of Asoka. Yet this furore of the dogs had no effect upon the camp. It appeared to be wrapped in slumber; no one came out to see who we were or what we were doing at that hour of the night. The only person we discovered who was not in a somnolent condition was a drunken Kalmuck, who hiccoughed in the orthodox fashion, and made futile efforts to calm the dogs. They were accustomed to him; but woe betide the stranger who might venture here alone, and on foot.

The dogs were a cross between a mastiff and a collie, standing as high as a small Shetland pony and as fierce as they were powerful. Prudence told me that the best refuge from them was to keep on horseback; I am sure that had we dismounted we should have had a bad time, for on the ground we should literally meet the dogs face to face—with all the advantage on their side.

By slow reconnaissance we found an empty aul, and aided by our newly-found, inebriated friend, took refuge inside.

The dogs bayed outside for a while, but did not attempt to cross the threshold; gradually they faded away, leaving us to rest, for we were far too tired to trouble about supper. I fell sound asleep and did not wake until the morning light was coming through the chinks of the aul. Outside the horses were neighing, and the booming of a gong told that the Buddhist priests were up and about, and that daylight had officially commenced.

The first thing I saw as I sat up and stretched myself, was a pair of wapiti stag horns, two large twelve-pointer heads, hanging up in the aul. This was the Asiatic Wapiti, one of the finest representatives of the deer family, his antlers constituting a record trophy. Among the Chinese the horns possess a medicinal value, when in the unformed state, being ground into powder and used for the cure of certain complaints. A good pair of antlers will fetch from ten to thirty pounds, so stag-hunting is profitable, and up to twenty-four have been bagged by one hunter in a month. As a result, the Asiatic Wapiti will soon have gone forever from the forests of the Tien Shan, just as the bison went from the prairies of North America.

I walked out into the camp of the Khan, to meet whom I had come so far and endured so much. Here it was, a forest of felt tents. This was the real thing ; a glimpse of old Tartary.

Presently the Khan's prime minister arrived to wish me a belated welcome. He was a cordial Kalmuck with a quiet dignity and all the charm and polish of a diplomat. He greeted me with easy courtesy, betokening pride of place and birth, for here was the chief minister of the descendant of Genghiz Khan. He apologized for my unofficial reception, which was due to his being unaware of my arrival.

This man controlled the destinies of a tribe based on thirteenth-century lines, where there is no distinction between the grades of society, and which has, above all, a link with the great Tartar overlords.

He put at my disposal a spacious aul, which was hung with embroideries. On the floor were carpets from Bokhara and Samarkand and cushions with coverings in Kalmuck needlework. Bedspreads and *rizais*, corresponding to our eiderdowns, completed the furnishings.

I had scarcely transferred my headquarters when breakfast was served—strips of mutton fried in fat and some tasty flour cakes, the flour a rare delicacy from China ; with it came tea worthy of Peking.

The prime minister told me there were about four hundred auls in the camp, and that those of the Khan and his entourage were within a large square. The Khan's were like large marquees, and here he lived in pavilioned splendour.

His auls were adorned with strips of red felt, giving a royal air to the tented town. In and near them were about fifty of the noisy fiends who had greeted us on arrival the night before. The dogs wore scarlet spiked collars as a sign of their royal connection. They were the giant version of our sheep dogs. A couple of them could tackle a lion, and three of them would have caused even the biggest tiger I have ever shot to think twice.

After breakfast the prime minister came to escort me to the Khan, and with two of my followers arrayed in their best we set out. Before me walked a retainer of the Khan bearing my Chinese visiting-card, a long strip of red paper showing my name and rank, or as near as the celestial writer could get to it. I was received at the royal apartments by a sort of chamberlain, and ushered into the durbar tent.

Never have I seen anything to compare with. the carpets in that tent. The durbar hall was hung with red cloth relieved here and there with embroideries, so that what with these and the gorgeous carpets and rugs there was a blaze of colour in comparison with which the tanned young Khan looked almost anæmic.

He was much interested in my expedition from India and asked many questions concerning that country and Tibet, for towards Tibet the Kalmuds, as Buddhists, turn a reverential eye.

The Khan enquired as to how many days' journey it would be to England if one went on horseback, a question that was somewhat of a poser, but to which I replied by saying it would take at least one hundred. This astonished him, for a Mongol visualizes all-out riding at a hundred miles a day, and it seemed too much. As he apparently doubted my accuracy I followed it up by assuring him that it would take much less if one went by Russian carriage (*droshky*) and rail. Unfortunately he knew nothing about railways, so this did not convey much. We had to return to the horse, the steed on which the Mongols rode to fame.

I had come prepared to be at a loss for suitable conversation and to fall back on the western, but not eastern, method of asking questions. But the Khan put all the questions!

After we had satisfactorily adjusted the matter of the distance to England, he went on to ask about my personal possessions. A patriarch himself, even at twenty-four, he was curious to know what was my own background, my houses, my oxen and asses— in fact, everything that was mine.

He was startled when I confessed I had no herds of cattle, sheep, and horses which I could call my own. To a Mongol, community life on the plains would be impossible without large herds of lambs, kine, and, above all, horses. These people still live in the days, not of medievalism, but of the Old Testament, when a leader was judged as much by the flocks that followed him as by the number of his followers.

My explanations here were obviously unsatisfactory, so I refrained from further comment ; but any future traveller to the land of the Kalmucks might remember this and prepare his words accordingly.

The Khan showed interest in India and appeared to know quite a lot about events there. This did not surprise me, for his emissaries went to and from India and, remote as he was from Hindustan, everything that happened there was known to him.

He could not understand how in India talkers and politicians held power, rather than warriors and the men on whom the actual safety of the country would depend. " A rifle can speak much farther than a man," he said, " and with greater accuracy."

But he was worried in his own mind about my personal possessions and, casting aside India, returned to this subject. So I felt that I must do something about it, and told him that my herds could not compare with his in size and quality. This had a magical effect, for when he saw that my kineless and sheepless poverty was not so great as he had been led to believe, his face lighted up. I at once enhanced the spirit of joy that came over him by adding that my father had a lordly mansion to make up for my other shortcomings, and that in this fabulous house there would be room for many of his great marquees to be stored away in corners.

Like the late Lord Curzon, who, when visiting the Amir of Afghanistan, was compelled to exalt himself in uniform and speech when it appeared that he might go down in the Afghan's estimation, I went all-out. I felt that, far away in Mongolia, Badminton and Chatsworth would forgive me for laying temporary claim to their glories.

We chatted on and he admired my rifle and shot-gun ; indeed, these were the things that gave a thrill to the Kalmucks.

I looked around the assembled company ; they were gathered in a semicircle behind the Khan, men in long felt riding boots with flapping garments—like great birds. This was a scene which would have been unchanged for Genghiz Khan, overlord of Asia and part of Europe, and of all the horse-riding Mongols from the Amur westward, when they rode out from the belt of High Asia in their bid for world dominion.

I could not help thinking that they may do so again, if they ever find another Genghiz or Tamerlane !

The Khan asked me what I thought of his people. I said we knew they were a branch of the great Mongols, magnificent riders, great hunters, unsurpassed on plain and hill and field. Anyone could see that these men and horses were undeniably one ; they could do anything they liked on horseback, including sleep there. They could charge, dodge, and alter course on their wiry horses as well as any in the world.

After the reception I returned to my aul and there held a *levée* at which there was a large attendance, for my arrival had caused excitement and curiosity.

My rifle and shot-gun were fingered lovingly, and then, after some hesitation, they started to bargain for them in Eastern fashion. First of all they offered me the finest horses in the camp : I could choose any three or four I desired : the choice was mine ; but I shook my head.

At this point two Kalmuck scouts arrived to report that bandits had raided the Khan's western boundaries and carried off a number of livestock. So everyone retired to make plans and send out an avenging force.

I stayed a day or two in the camp, in the course of which I heard this story.

On reaching the age of twenty-five the Khan vanishes from this world and a new Khan reigns in his stead. The mode of his disappearance is obscure, but apparently the end is brought about by poison. I never ascertained the origin of this custom, but was told that a former Khan, whose views on the subject differed from those of the priests and elders, not wishing to qualify for an early death, had fled from the cares of state on nearing the fatal age.

As I rode away from the Khan's camp to the westward, I thought how uneasy lies the head that wears a crown in the land of the Kalmucks and the descendants of the great Genghiz.

TIMES AND SEASONS

Two hundred miles to the north of the Khan's camp are the Altai Mountains, once the private property of the Tsar of Russia.

Some years after my visit, a discussion began at a dinner party to try to decide the coldest place on earth. A Russian professor of science told us that the honour belongs to the Yakutsk district of Siberia, where, after long and close scientific observation, the thermometer beat all records by dropping to ninety-three degrees below zero. Perhaps at some other point in this desperately cold land it may fall a degree or two lower, but I think the above figure will be low enough for most people.

When I was in north-western Mongolia, on the borders of the Altai and Siberia, I found the winter was almost frightening in its severity. This zone of shivering is intensified by the cold winds and blizzards that sweep the country. Here horse and camel are kings, while the dogs, too, play a useful part.

The Mongol dog is a companion, when he gets to know you. There are no other domestic creatures, such as poultry—for they exist merely to crow in the imagination because they have been talked about by travellers from the world outside—and no one ever sees a cat. Indeed, I was told that cats cannot live above six or seven thousand feet, although on the Afghan border of Russia I once came across a cat who was very cordial and friendly at just under twelve thousand feet altitude—so there must be something wrong in the Mongol calculations.

During the winter the ground in this part of the Gobi is a natural ice-box, and so the inhabitants catch fish in the summer, which they bury in trenches for use in winter, the fish being used for both man and dog. The Mongols never ill-treat their dogs ; they know each other's dogs by name, and a leading topic of conversation is the quality as well as the value of horses and dogs and camels.

I was always impressed with the sagacity of the Mongol canine friends ; they have a remarkable bump of locality. In the winter when the storms are on and to all intents and purposes a man appears to be absolutely lost in this immense white wilderness, without landmarks of any description to guide him or give the slightest indication of his whereabouts, the dogs will head unerringly for the camp that is home.

Travelling in this realm of cold becomes a chilly, ghostly progress. The stillness is uncanny and the barking of the dogs when they come within sight of habitation sounds like an echo in a vast void that has died in its sleep.

The road goes on interminably ; habitations are only met with at intervals of one hundred and fifty or two hundred miles. When one point on the horizon is reached there is still the same straight stretch of country ahead, the same horizon without end.

Suddenly a camp looms up on the horizon like the figure of hope, and as it comes in sight the dogs begin to bark joyously. I always share their joy to the full, thawing slowly from outer darkness into the warmth of light and life.

The western Mongols are hospitable to the stranger within their gates. Living a life of warfare with the elements they are a law unto themselves.

When someone arrives from outside he is treated as the guest of honour, for does he not bring news of what may be happening in a dim and distant country beyond the reach of their nimblest thoughts ? He is at once given the warmest place by the fire, is treated to all the tit-bits of steak and marrow bone, and is questioned as to the performance of his horses, the speed at which they cover the ground, and their relative qualities in comparison with the village teams. In fact, conversation turns almost at once to matters of purely local interest ; surely this is the kind of place, above all others, where gossip and story-telling can be excused.

As night closes over the lonely little camp, lamps are lighted— earthenware bowls filled with oil, giving off an appalling smoke and very little in the way of illumination. In the flickering light the principal meal of the day is then taken. It will probably consist of boiled horseflesh, fish boiled or baked in the sun, with the main course of marrow and a slice of mutton.

Time with these people counts for nothing. One day is very much like the next, yet they have an unusual system of recording time : their primitive calendar is cut on a long stick, each day having its notch, the notches correspondingly larger for a fête day.

Their yourts or auls are the common home of the family and the dogs, and the smell permeating these movable homes is so strong that the visitor is staggered. Tent odour can possess almost the force of a blow and would make a horse pause, but it helps, no doubt, to keep the inmates warm and sustained with the illusion of comfort.

As I have remarked elsewhere, these more primitive Mongols dislike soap and water ; in fact, soap is quite unknown, and they are said to wash only twice in a lifetime, once at birth, when the child is supposed to enter the world pure and undefiled, and again on the eve of marriage.

A Mongol wears his clothes until they drop or let in the cold so much that he is forced to renovate them. A garment that lasts a lifetime is held in high esteem, and the wearer regarded as worthy of public recognition. A Mongol tailor could announce with pride that he makes suits that will live. It is strange to think that these people are in close contact with luxuries which can only be purchased, especially out of season, at high prices in Europe. For instance, caviare they largely discard, and quantities of it will be seen lying along the shores of the Zaisan Lake ; several sacks could be filled within an hour.

Severe though the winter is, and harrowing its experience, there is always the spring to look forward to. Only those who have gone through the death-grip of winter can realize what the spring really means.

The first stirrings occur early in March. The thermometer is only a few degrees below zero, and the sun, which has been mostly hidden for the last five or six months, now suddenly appears. It shines in all its glory, warmth, and brilliance ; there is nothing in the tropics or elsewhere to compare with such a sight : the yellow orb rises majestically every morning amid the vast shimmering expanse of snow, filling the clear blue sky of unending distances with such dazzle and brilliance that one needs strong blue glasses. What an event this is in the life of the people ! They watch for the first view of the sun rising slowly in power above the horizon, and those who first see it are supposed to come into much good fortune. In fact, many a person in this chilly zone worships the sun, falling on his knees and rendering deep obeisance for all the blessings which it brings.

Wonderful and welcome indeed are these first signs of spring ; all at once the tingling atmosphere turns warm, the slabs of ice grow thinner, the ice cracks and reverberates, rivers and streams start to roar, and the floes grind themselves out on their long journey to the Arctic Ocean, two thousand miles away.

The winter, as if putting forth a last despairing effort, resents the thaw, and a time of violent storms usually sets in ; snowdrifts are piled up, whirling currents of snow twist through the air, and the wind howls dismally round the felt tents.

Gradually spring asserts itself. Geese arrive from the far south. The geese are the real harbingers of spring ; they have come from the lakes and rivers of India, the marshlands of Northern Australia, even from distant Southern China and Siam, cleaving the air like arrows. They have flown anything from six to twelve thousand miles back to the land of their origin.

With them are the gulls ; the week before they have been wheeling and circling over Gibraltar, or the Golden Horn, or the Dalmatian coast. Now they are in the Gobi.

One of the most interesting bird migrants is the roseate gull, with iris-coloured beak and legs and a greyish body. It is one of the rarer gulls and is not often seen except in the spring migration.

Seebohm asserted that bird-life started in the Arctic and that it is the nursery of nearly all birds.

Now come the flowers : unexpected daffodils and a kind of bluebell, together with moss speckled with white flowers like lilies of the valley. The smell of flowers, the moss, and the soft breeze remind one of a forest glade in temperate climes. It is all so unlike the Gobi of popular imagination.

All life is stirring now: the call of the geese in the early morning keeps one awake, the chatter of smaller birds indicates that domestic cares and responsibilities are being talked over.

The tiny camps, which throughout the long winter were dormant, are now hives of industry. The men are driving the flocks to spring pastures, and they visit the fox-traps which have been set in the winter months—deadfalls of timber supported by a prop which, when the fox capsizes it, crushes him instantly to death. The women are collecting argol, and the driftwood which floats down the rivers. This driftwood, worth its weight in gold, is collected and stored along the river bank, each log bearing the special mark of ownership of the family to which it belongs. Honesty and good faith are strong points in the character of these nomads, children of obscure descent, and no one will ever steal a stick of wood that bears the mark of another.

Thieves are rare here; the traveller journeying hundreds of miles away from home may decide to leave some of his property by the roadside if he finds the load beginning to tell and his ponies and camels unable to cope with it. He leaves the things rolled up in a neatly stacked heap by the trackside, forming a cloakroom of his own choosing. It may be months before he retrieves his goods, but nothing will be missing.

The Mongol leaves his aul unguarded and may be away a week or a fortnight. He lets down the felt hanging that serves for a doorway, places food and drink for the wayfarer who may appear, and rides away, knowing that nothing will be stolen, and, if it is, that the robber will be hunted down and given the swift justice of the desert.

When travelling with the Mongols I always noticed that they never said right or left, but east or west. Then I remembered that long before Europe ever heard of it the Chinese had discovered and used the compass and the Mongols had acquired the habit of referring to the points of the compass when on the move. With this knowledge they merged that of the sun, moon, and stars. Through the daylight they watched the skies; through the darkness they peered out over the desert and measured time and distance, reckoning from the worlds above them.

They seemed to know exactly where to go. They knew and spoke with awe of parts of the desert that must be avoided, and told of explorers who had penetrated the inner Gobi and unearthed remains of settlements that existed long ages ago. These are far off among the endless dunes, buried by the sand.

These once flourishing cities were engulfed by a process of encroachment. At first the walls of the houses kept out the advance guard of the sand, but gradually it climbed over them. Then the courtyards were invaded, until by the impact of successive storms, the drifts mounted to the roofs and completed the work of destruction.

These cities were built of sun-dried bricks, and a kind of matting was used in the foundations. Sheets of this matting are sometimes found beneath the walls, parts of which are in a good state of preservation, although they date back for at least three thousand years. An archæological expert discovered a foot rule with the cord, by which to hang it up, still attached. It was divided like a French rule on the decimal principle, while pieces of pottery looked so new that they might have been made but yesterday.

Such places of a bygone age assume an irregular form silhouetted against the horizon at sundown. On all sides is the indefinite, overhanging blackness of the sandhills, with the yellow sand beneath.

In the gathering gloom the Mongols hasten through these sinister places ; they are the abode of the evil ones. Nothing would ever induce them to camp there : "for the spirits of the lost pass up and down in the still hours of the night and it is death to hear them."

I could appreciate their fears, for here, as in the Sahara, noises and tunes are heard that baffle description, noises, caused by action of the wind on the sand, that sound like sirens. Marco Polo when he passed by seven hundred years ago listened to this noise.

That, then, is the mystic and magical Gobi, with its glamorous and historical past, its isolated present, and a future of which no man can tell.

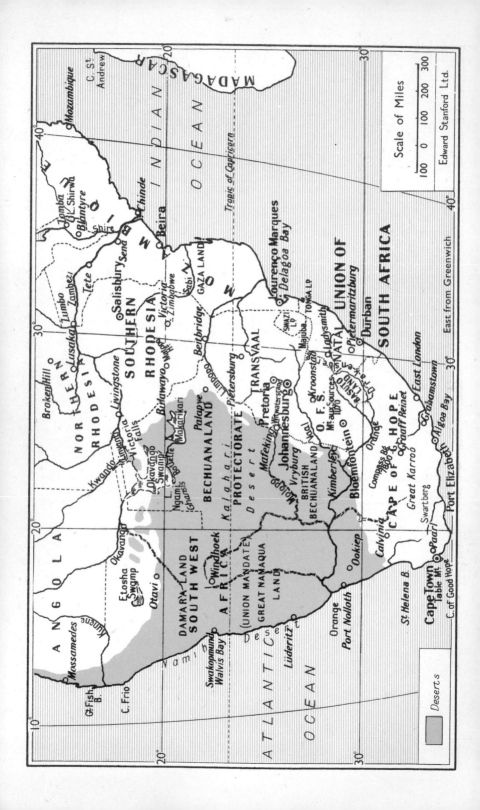